The easiest way to learn Hindi (or any other language) is to hear it spoken. This book, designed by a successful teacher of Hindi to foreigners, creates an 'audio' effect for quicker grasp and assimilation. Rules of grammar have been explained only where absolutely necessary. A direct conversational style, with the help of a minimal vocabulary, makes learning Hindi effortless and pleasurable.

Correct pronunciation is difficult, specially for tongues not accustomed to the Devanagri script. Diacritical marks have been provided to indicate different sounds and accents. By regular practice, with the help of this book, one can acquire a working knowledge of spoken and written Hindi.

Mohini Rao, former editor, National Book Trust, has taught Hindi to foreigners for many years--at the American Embassy, and at the Hindi Institute run by herself.

# TEACH YOURSELF HINDI

Mohini Rao

HIND POCKET BOOKS

TEACH YOURSELF HINDI

This edition, 1999
ISBN 81-216-0192-4

Published by
**Hind Pocket Books (P) Ltd.**
18-19, Dilshad Garden, G.T. Road
Delhi-110 095

Designing, Typesetting & Print Production : SCANSET
18-19, Dilshad Garden, G.T., Road, Delhi-110 095
Tel: 228 2467, 229 7792, 93, 94 Fax: 228 2332

Printed at Jain Composing Agency, Delhi-110032

PRINTED IN INDIA

# FOREWORD

There are several books on the subject of learning Hindi without a guide or a teacher. One can only learn the basic rules of grammar and a minimal vocabulary from a book for everyday use.

The basic vocabulary needed by a person may vary according to his interest or occupation. I have tried to give in this book phrases and sentences used commonly. A minimal dictionary has also been added at the end. Rules of grammar have been explained only where absolutely necessary, for I believe that hearing a language constantly and attentively is the best way of learning it.

A book, even the best one, can help only in a limited way if the language is not heard regularly and spoken without inhibition.

Hindi is a phonetic language. It is written as it is spoken. The reader is advised to learn the script from the beginning as it shortens the process of learning and also helps pronounce correctly.

There are some sounds in Hindi which cannot be reproduced accurately in the Roman script.

This book teaches you the spoken Hindi, popularly known as Hindustani which is a pleasant mixture of Hindi and Urdu words which are understood commonly. The key to the pronunciation and the phonetic symbols should be followed as accurately as possible.

In the end I would like to add that the method adopted in this book is based on my own vast personal experience of teaching Hindi to foreigners, and it is an attempt only to teach the rudiments of the language.

I should be happy if this little book benefits both foreigners and Indians who wish to learn Hindi the easy way.

New Delhi *Mohini Rao*

# CONTENTS

CHAPTER ONE

# KEY TO PRONUNCIATION

## Phonetic Symbols

This sign over a letter stands for a long vowel sound. For example,

*ā* to be pronounced as aa.

*ī* to be pronounced as ee.

Mark the difference between *a* and *ā*, *i* and *ī* ~~and~~ *u* and *ū*.

Pronounce it loudly many times to get the desired result.

˜ This symbol over a letter denotes a nasalized sound. For example, *ñ* would be pronounced as n with a nasal sound and not as a separate consonant.

. A dot under a letter denotes the hard and aspirated form of a particular consonant. For example,

*d*—soft dental sound as in *dāl* (lentils)

*ḍ*—hard cerebral sound as in *ḍar* (fear)

*dh*—soft aspirated form as in *dūdh* (milk)

*ḍh*—hard aspirated form as in *ḍholak* (drum)

**Vowels**

There are twelve vowels in Hindi

| | | |
|---|---|---|
| अ | *a* | as in *u*ltra |
| आ | *ā* | as in f*a*ther |
| इ | *i* | as in *i*nk, p*i*nk |
| ई | *ī* | as in f*ee*l, n*ee*d |
| उ | *u* | as in p*u*ll, b*u*ll |
| ऊ | *ū* | as in m*oo*n, t*oo*l |
| ए | *ē* | as in r*ay*, g*ay* |
| ऐ | *ai* | as in a̲ngle |
| ओ | *ō* | as in s*o*, *o*ver |
| औ | *au* | as in c*o*llege |
| अं | *ang* | as in h*u*nger |
| अः | *ah* | as in *a*h |

(–अ is also written as ॠ)

**Consonants**

There are thirty-six consonants.

| | | |
|---|---|---|
| क | *ka* | as in kite |
| ख | *kha* | aspirated *ka* |
| ग | *ga* | as in go |
| घ | *gha* | aspirated *ga* |
| ङ | *nga* | *as* in stung |
| च | *cha* | as in chair |
| छ | *chha* | aspirated *cha* |
| ज | *ja* | as in jar |
| झ | *jha* | aspirated *ja* |
| ञ | *ṇa* | no equivalant sound in English. |
| ट | *ṭa* | as in talk |

| | | |
|---|---|---|
| ठ | *ṭha* | aspirated *ṭa* |
| ड | *ḍa* | as in dog |
| ढ | *ḍha* | aspirated *ḍa* |
| ण | *ṇa* | This sound does not exist in English |
| त | *ta* | soft dental sound. Not used in English |
| थ | *tha* | aspirated *ta* |
| द | *da* | soft dental sound. Not used in English. |
| ध | *dha* | aspirated *da* |
| न | *na* | as in nose |
| प | *pa* | as in pulp |
| फ | *pha* | aspirated *pa* |
| ब | *ba* | as in bun |
| भ | *bha* | aspirated *ba* |
| म | *ma* | as in mother |
| य | *ya* | as in yellow |
| र | *ra* | as in rubber |
| ल | *la* | as in lull |
| व | *va* | as in verb |
| श | *sha* | as in shudder |
| ष | *ṣha* | Since the distinction between श and ष is very subtle, and the sound almost the same, both the letters are represented here by the Roman letters *sha*. To mark the distinction in the written form, a dot has been added under ṣ in the case of ष । Beginners need not worry too much about this as ष is not used often. |
| स | *sa* | as in sulk |
| ह | *ha* | as in hunger |
| क्ष | *ksha* | no equivalent sound in English. |

| | | |
|---|---|---|
| त्र | *tra* | as in truck with a soft dental t. |
| ज्ञ | *jña* | no equivalent sound in English. |

**Consonants at a Glance**

| | | | | |
|---|---|---|---|---|
| क | ख | ग | घ | ङ |
| *ka* | *kha* | *ga* | *gha* | *nga* |
| च | छ | ज | झ | ञ |
| *cha* | *chha* | *ja* | *jha* | *yan* |
| ट | ठ | ड | ढ | ण |
| *ṭa* | *tha* | *ḍa* | *ḍha* | *ṇa* |
| त | थ | द | ध | न |
| *ta* | *tha* | *da* | *dha* | *na* |
| प | फ | ब | भ | म |
| *pa* | *pha* | *ba* | *bha* | *ma* |
| य | र | ल | व | |
| *ya* | *ra* | *la* | *va* | |
| श | ष | स | ह | |
| *sha* | *ṣha* | *sa* | *ha* | |
| क्ष | त्र | ज्ञ | | |
| *ksha* | *tra* | *jña* | | |

You will notice that the two sets of consonants ट, ठ, ड, ढ and त, थ, द, ध have been represented by the same set of *ta, tha, da* and *dha*. (see the third and fourth rows above). To mark the difference in pronunciation the soft dental consonants त, थ, द, ध have been represented by *ta, tha, da* and *dha* and the second set of the hard consonants have a dot under them, as explained earlier in the paragraph on phonetic symbols.

It is important to understand this not only to help in the correct pronunciation, but to be able to distinguish one sound from another, as two words like *dāl* and *ḍāl* have entirely different meanings. (*dāl* means lentils and *ḍāl* a branch of a tree).

There are two more letters ड़ and its aspirated form ढ़ which are used very often. They will be written in the Roman script here as *ḍa* (ड़) and *ḍha* (ढ़).

F and Z have been adapted into the Hindi alphabet. These sounds are acquired by adding a dot under फ *pha* and ज ja.

For example :

| | | | | | |
|---|---|---|---|---|---|
| फ | *pha* | *phal* (fruit) | ज | *ja* | *jānā* (to go) |
| फ़ | *fa* | *fasal* (crop) | ज़ | *za* | *zarūr* (certainly) |

**Aspirated and Unaspirated Consonants**

Consonants are of two types, aspirated and unaspirated. The difference in sound is the presence or absence of a breath of air after the initial consonant. In the *Varṇamālā* each aspirated consonant follows the unaspirated form.

| Unaspirated | | Aspirated | | Unaspirated | | Aspirated | |
|---|---|---|---|---|---|---|---|
| क | *ka* | ख | *kha* | ड | *ḍa* | ढ | *ḍha* |
| ग | *ga* | घ | *gha* | त | *ta* | थ | *tha* |
| च | *cha* | छ | *chha* | द | *da* | ध | *dha* |
| ज | *ja* | झ | *jha* | प | *pa* | फ | *pha* |
| ट | *ṭa* | ठ | *ṭha* | ब | *ba* | भ | *bha* |

In English most consonants are pronounced with aspiration. It is therefore more difficult for English speaking people to pronounce the soft dental or the unaspirated consonants correctly.

One of the most effective ways of being sure of pronouncing the aspirated and unaspirated consonants correctly is to hold a paper or a handkerchief in front of your mouth. When an aspirated consonant is pronounced the paper or the handkerchief will shake slightly. It will remain steady when a consonant is not aspirated. It is very important not only to know the difference while pronouncing, **but also to know the difference while hearing.**

The vowel *a* is inherent in each consonant, and that is why क has been wirtten as *ka*. The *a* in a consonant is absent only when it is combined with a vowel or when it forms a conjunct with another consonant, e.g., when *ka* क is combined with *ī* it becomes *kī* की ।

The last three letters in the alphabet are compound consonants.

| | | | |
|---|---|---|---|
| क्ष | *ksha* | is | *ka+sha* |
| त्र | *tra* | is | *ta+ra* |
| ज्ञ | *jña* | is | *ja+na* |

**Complete *Varṇamālā* (alphabet) at a glance**

| | | | | | | | | |
|---|---|---|---|---|---|---|---|---|
| अ | आ | इ | ई | उ | ऊ | ऋ | ए | ऐ |
| *a* | *ā* | *i* | *ī* | *u* | *ū* | *ri* | *ē* | *ai* |
| ओ | औ | अं | अः | | | | | |
| *ō* | *au* | *an* | *ah* | | | | | |

| | | | | |
|---|---|---|---|---|
| क | ख | ग | घ | ङ |
| *ka* | *kha* | *ga* | *gha* | *nga* |
| च | छ | ज | झ | ञ |
| *cha* | *chha* | *ja* | *jha* | *yan* |
| ट | ठ | ड | ढ | ण |
| *ṭa* | *ṭha* | *ḍa* | *ḍha* | *ṇa* |
| त | थ | द | ध | न |
| *ta* | *tha* | *da* | *dha* | *na* |
| प | फ | ब | भ | म |
| *pa* | *pha* | *ba* | *bha* | *ma* |
| य | र | ल | व | |
| *ya* | *ra* | *la* | *va* | |
| श | ष | स | ह | |
| *sha* | *ṣha* | *sa* | *ha* | |
| क्ष | त्र | ज्ञ | | |
| *ksha* | *tra* | *jña* | | |

**Vowel Signs or *mātrā***

A vowel is written as a complete letter only when it is used in *the begining of a word e.g.*, आना व आओ । When it accurs in the middle or at the end of a word it is combined with a consonant. This may be called the vowel sign or *mātrā* e.g. खाना, खीरा । A vowel sign is called *mātrā* in Hindi.

**A vowel is pronounced by itself but a vowel sign is pronounced together with a consonant.** Each vowel is represented by a sign or *mātrā* as given in the following pages. It is also shown here how it is combined with a consonant in the script.

| *Vowel* | | *Sign or* mātrā | *as Combined with a consonant* | *Example* | |
|---|---|---|---|---|---|
| अ | *(a)* | has no vowel sign as it is inherent in a consonant | | कमर | *kamar* |
| आ | *(ā)* | ा | क+आ=का<br>*ka+ā=kā* | काला | *kālā* (black) |
| इ | *(i)* | ि | क+इ=कि<br>*ka+i=ki* | किताब | *kitāb* (book) |
| ई | *(ī)* | ी | क+ई=की<br>*ka+ī=kī* | कीमा | *kīmā* (mince-meat) |
| उ | *(u)* | ु | क+उ=कु<br>*ka+u=ku* | कुरता | *kurtā* (Indian shirt) |
| ऊ | *(ū)* | ू | क+ऊ=कू<br>*ka+ū=kū* | कूद | *kūd* (jump) |

| | | | | | |
|---|---|---|---|---|---|
| ए | (*ē*) | के | क+ए=के<br>*ka+ē=kē* | केला | *kēlā* (banana) |
| ऐ | (*ai*) | कै | क+ऐ=कै<br>*ka+ai=kai* | कैसा | *kaisā* (how) |
| ओ | (*ō*) | ो | क+औ=को<br>ka+ō=kō | कोना | *kōnā* (corner) |
| औ | (*au*) | ौ | क+औ=कौ<br>*ka+au= kau* | कौन | *kaun* (who) |
| अं | (*an*) | | क+अ=कं<br>*ka+an=kan* | कंघी | *kañghī* (comb) |

Note : A nasal sound at the end of a word has been shown thus : *kahañ*. It would be a good exercise to write this out combining the *mātrā* with different consonants as on the next page.

| | | | | | | | | | | | |
|---|---|---|---|---|---|---|---|---|---|---|---|
| क | का | कि | की | कु | कू | के | कै | को | कौ | कं | कः |
| *ka* | *kā* | *ki* | *kī* | *ku* | *kū* | *kē* | *kai* | *kō* | *kau* | *kan* | *kah* |
| ख | खा | खि | खी | खु | खू | खे | खै | खो | खौ | खं | खः |
| *kha* | *khā* | *khi* | *khī* | *khu* | *khū* | *khē* | *khai* | *khō* | *khau* | *khañ* | *khah* |
| ग | गा | गि | गी | गु | गू | गे | गै | गो | गौ | गं | गः |
| *ga* | *gā* | *gi* | *gī* | *gu* | *gū* | *gē* | *gai* | *gō* | *gau* | *gañ* | *gah* |
| घ | घा | घि | घी | घु | घू | घे | घै | घो | घौ | घं | घः |
| *gha* | *ghā* | *ghi* | *ghī* | *ghu* | *ghū* | *ghē* | *ghai* | *ghō* | *ghau* | *ghañ* | *ghah* |
| च | चा | चि | ची | चु | चू | चे | चै | चो | चौ | चं | चः |
| *cha* | *chā* | *chi* | *chī* | *chu* | *chū* | *chē* | *chai* | *chō* | *chau* | *chañ* | *chah* |
| छ | छा | छि | छी | छु | छू | छे | छै | छो | छौ | छं | छः |
| *chha* | *chhā* | *chhi* | *chhī* | *chhu* | *chhū* | *chhē* | *chhai* | *chhō* | *chhau* | *chhañ* | *chhah* |
| ज | जा | जि | जी | जु | जू | जे | जै | जो | जौ | जं | जः |
| *ja* | *jā* | *ji* | *jī* | *ju* | *jū* | *jē* | *jai* | *jō* | *jau* | *jañ* | *jah* |

And so on. This exercise would be of immense help particularly to those who are learning to read and write.

## Conjunct Consonants

Two consonants are combined in this manner :

क + ख = क्क

क + ख = क्ख

ग + ग = ग्ग

च + छ = च्छ

Another way of joining two consonants is to add a stroke under the first one. This may be easier until you have had a good practice in writing.

क + क = क्‌क

Consonants in Hindi are of two types :

(i) those which have a vertical line in the end, and

(ii) those which do not have a vertical line.

The following consonants come under the first type :

| | | | | | | |
|---|---|---|---|---|---|---|
| क | ख | ग | घ | च | ज | झ |
| ञ | ण | त | ध | घ | न | प |
| फ | ब | भ | म | य | ल | व |
| श | ष | स | क्ष | त्र | ज्ञ | |

र is joined with another consonant in this manner :

| | | |
|---|---|---|
| कर्म | *karma* | act, action |
| क्रम | *krama* | order, sequence |
| कृपा | *kripā* | kindness |

1. In the first instance, *karma, ra* comes before the last letter *ma* (*ka+rma*) and appears in the form of a hook ( ॅ ) on

the top of the letter which follows it.

2. In the second example, *krama, ra* is joined to the first consonant *ka (kra + ma)* and is in the form of a stroke (क्र) under it.

3. In the third word, *kripā, ra* and *i* (*ri*) are joined to *ka*. When *ra* is combined with *i* in a conjunct, it is symbolized with ृ under the consonant to which it is joined.

The form कृ or नृ etc. are essentially from Sanskrit and used only in Sanskrit words which have been adopted in Hindi. If you were to write a word like British in *Devanāgrī*, the correct way of writing would be ब्रिटिश and not बृटिश.

क and त are joined as क्त. There is a change of style now, but when you see क्त you should know it is *kta* conjunct.

It has been mentioned earlier that every consonant has an *a* in it, but it has purposely been added at the end of words ending in consonants to avoid mistakes in pronunciation. Sometimes names are pronounced with an *ā* ending even if there is no such sound at the end. There cannot be a better example than the prevalent mispronunciation, even by Indians of *Ashokā* Hotel. The name of the great Hindu emperor was Ashoka, after whom the hotel is named. But it is usually pronounced with a long *ā* at the end. This pronunciation has come to stay. But when there are two consonants in the middle of a word, the vowel 'a' is written between them in the Roman script to avoid mistaking them as conjunct consonants.

## Syntax

The verb in Hindi is always placed at the end of a sentence, for example,

I go to school will be *maĩñ skūl jātā hūñ* (I to school go) in Hindi.

मेरा नाम राम है। *mērā nām Rām hai*

(My name Ram is)

मेरा घर बड़ा है। *mērā ghar baḍā hai*

My house big is

The preposition in Hindi is actually a post-position. For example, in English it is said : *the book is on the table.* In Hindi it would be : *kitāb mēz par hai* (book table on is). पर *par* (on) is placed after *mēz* (table) and not before.

Similarly, *gilās mēñ pāni hai* (glass in water is).

In an interrogative sentence the position are as follows :

Where do you live ?

*āp kahāñ rahatē haiñ ?*

You where live ?

A simple question is often indicated by the tone and not by changing the placement of the verb as is done in English. For example *āpkā nām kyā hai ?* (What is your name ?) is clear as an interrogation as indicated by *kyā* (what). But in a sentence such as *āpkā nām Rām hai ?* (Is your name Ram ?) the question is indicated only by the tone.

Sometimes the meaning is changed if the syntax is changed.

For example,

*āp kyā khāeñgē ?* (What will you eat ?)

*kyā āp khāeñgē ?* (Will you eat ?)

CHAPTER TWO

# NOUNS

## संज्ञा *(Sangyā)*

### Gender (लिंग *linga*)

There are only two genders in Hindi--masculine (*puling* पुलिंग) and feminine (*strīling* स्त्रीलिंग). Gender is based either on sex (in the case of human beings and animals) or on usage. There are no hard and fast rules. According to the general rule, all words ending with the vowel sound *ā* are masculine and those ending with the vowel sound *ī* are feminine. Words ending in a consonant may be masculine or feminine. But there are many exceptions to this rule which you will learn as you proceed. It may be pointed out here that the gender is the weakest point of Hindi grammar. This should not discourage learners as they should know at the very outset that if they take time in mastering the gender in Hindi, it is because of the arbitrary rules of the grammar which are established more or less by usage. Some examples of common masculine and feminine nouns are given here :

**Masculine nouns ending with the vowel *ā***

| | | |
|---|---|---|
| रुपया | *rupyā* | rupee |
| केला | *kēlā* | banana |
| संतरा | *santarā* | orange |

| | | |
|---|---|---|
| कमरा | *kamarā* | room |
| लड़का | *laḍkā* | boy |
| बेटा | *bēṭā* | son |

**Masculine nouns ending with a consonant**

| | | |
|---|---|---|
| घर | *ghar* | home or house |
| मकान | *makān* | house |
| मंदिर | *mandir* | temple |
| चावल | *chāval* | rice |
| फल | *phal* | fruit |
| फूल | *phūl* | flower |

**Exceptional masculine nouns which end with the vowel *ī***

| | | |
|---|---|---|
| आदमी | *ādamī* | man |
| हाथी | *hāthī* | elephant |
| पानी | *pānī* | water |
| घी | *ghī* | clarified butter |
| पति | *pati* | husband |

**Feminine nouns ending with the vowel *ī***

| | | |
|---|---|---|
| लड़की | *laḍkī* | girl |
| बेटी | *bēṭī* | daughter |
| पत्नी | *patnī* | wife |
| चीनी | chīnī | sugar |
| साड़ी | *sāṛī* | saree |

**Feminine nouns ending with a consonant**

| | | |
|---|---|---|
| औरत | *aurat* | woman |
| कलम | *kalam* | pen |
| किताब | *kitāb* | book |
| मेज़ | *mēz* | table |

**Feminine nouns ending with the vowel *ā***

| | | |
|---|---|---|
| हवा | *havā* | wind, air |
| दवा | *davā* | medicine |

The absence of a neuter gender may cause some confusion in the mind of learners, e. g., while *chāval* (rice) is masculine, *roṭi* (bread) is feminine, *kān* (ear) is masculine but *nāk* (nose) is feminine. *dāñt* (tooth) is masculine but *jībhi* (tongue) is feminine. Nouns belonging to the same subject or of the same goup like the different parts of the body, or different fruits or vegetables have different genders. As pointed out earlier, this can be learnt only though regular and uninhibited practice in speaking and attentive hearing.

In most cases a masculine noun can be converted into a feminine noun by changing the *ā* into *ī* ending.

Examples

| Masculine | | Feminine | |
|---|---|---|---|
| लड़का | *laḍka* | लड़की | *laḍkī* |
| बेटा | *bēṭā* | बेटी | *bēṭī* |

Sometimes the feminine gender is used to indicate the diminutive form of an object, e. g., थाल *thāl;* (a big metal plate for eating) becomes थाली *thālī;* कटोरा *kaṭōrā* (a big bowl) becomes कटोरी *kaṭōrī* (a small bowl).

**Number** (वचन *vachan*)

In the case of common nouns, the plural form is formed by the following rules:

**i) Masculine nouns with *ā* ending**

| | | | | | |
|---|---|---|---|---|---|
| | Singular (एकवचन *ekvachan*) | | | Plural (बहुवचन *bahuvachan*) | |
| लड़का | *laḍkā* | (boy) | लड़के | *laḍkē* | (boys) |
| बेटा | *bēṭā* | (son) | बेटे | bēṭē | (sons) |

**ii) Masculine nouns ending with a consonant or any other vowel except *ā*, do not change in the plural form**

| | | |
|---|---|---|
| आदमी | *ādmī* | man |
| चाकू | *chākū* | knife |
| सेब | *sēb* | apple |
| मकान | *makān* | house |
| फल | *phal* | fruit |
| फूल | *phūl* | flower |

**iii) Feminine nouns ending with *ī* are changed into plural by adding *yāñ* in the end, e. g.**

| | | | | | |
|---|---|---|---|---|---|
| | Singular | | | Plural | |
| लड़की | *laḍkī* | (girl) | लड़कियां | *laḍkiyāñ* | (girls) |
| बेटी | *bēṭi* | (daughter) | बेटियां | *bēṭiyāñ* | (daughters) |

**iv) Feminine nouns with consonant ending are changed into plural form by adding *ēñ* to the last consonant, e. g.**

| | | | | | |
|---|---|---|---|---|---|
| | Singular | | | Plural | |
| किताब | *kitāb* | (book) | किताबें | *kitābēñ* | (books) |
| औरत | *aurat* | (woman) | औरतें | *auratēñ* | (women) |

The gender and the number of the subject govern the qualifying adjective and the verb. The adjective and the verb also decline accordingly (explained in detail in the chapters on adjectives and verbs). Let us make some simple sentences.

| | | |
|---|---|---|
| यह लड़का है। | *yah laḍkā hai* | This is a boy. |
| यह लड़की है। | *yah ladkī hai* | This is a girl. |
| यह लड़का सुन्दर है। | *yah laḍkā sundar hai* | This boy is a handsome. |
| यह लड़की सुन्दर है। | *yah laḍkī sundar hai* | This girl is a pretty. |
| यह लड़का छोटा है। | *yah laḍkā chhōtā hai* | This boy is small. |
| यह लड़की छोटी है। | *yah laḍkī chhōṭī hai* | This girl is small. |

Let us first get the construction of the sentence clear. *Yāh laḍkā hai,* translated literally would mean *this boy is.* As explained in the beginning, the verb always comes at the end of a sentence.

The adjective *sundar* did not change in the case of *laḍkī* as the word ends with a consonant. It does not decline with the number or gender. But the adjective *chhōtā* became *chhōṭī* in the case of a girl because of the long *ā* ending. You will now understand how important the end sound is.

The auxiliary verbs *hai* (is) or *haiñ* (are) do not change with gender. Let us have some more sentences to make this point clear.

| | | |
|---|---|---|
| यह घर बड़ा है। | *yah ghar baḍā hai* | This house is big. |
| ये घर बड़े हैं। | *yē ghar baḍē haiñ* | These houses are big. |
| यह कमरा छोटा है। | *yah kamrā chhōṭā* | This room is small. |
| ये कमरे छोटे हैं। | *yē kamrā chhōte haiñ* | These rooms are small. |
| ये कमरे बड़े हैं। | *yē kamrē baṛē haiñ* | These rooms are big. |

| | | |
|---|---|---|
| यह रोटी है। | *yah rōṭī hai* | This is a bread. |
| ये रोटियां हैं। | *yē rōṭiyañ haiñ* | These are breads. |
| यह रोटी गरम है। | *yah rōṭī garam hai* | This bread is hot. |
| ये रोटियां गरम हैं। | *yē rōṭiyañ garam haiñ* | These breads are hot. |
| यह रोटी गरम नहीं हैं। | *yah rōṭi garam nahīñ hai* | This bread is not hot. |
| ये रोटियां गरम नहीं हैं। | *yē rōṭiyañ garam nahīñ haiñ* | These breads are not hot. |
| पानी ठंडा है। | *pānī ṭhanḍa hai* | The water is cold. |
| पानी ठंडा नहीं है। | *pānī ṭhanḍa nahīñ hai* | The water is not cold. |
| कमरा गरम है। | *kamarā garam hai* | The room is hot. |
| कमरा गरम नहीं है। | *kamarā garam nahīñ hai* | The room is not hot. |

**Vocabulary**

| | | |
|---|---|---|
| गरम | *garam* | hot, warm |
| ठंडा | *ṭhanḍā* | cold |
| नहीं | *nahīñ* | not, no |
| है | *hai* | is |
| हैं | *haiñ* | are |

**Articles**

Note that there are no definite or indefinite articles in Hindi. Also note the placing of *nahīñ* in the above sentences.

CHAPTER THREE

# CASES AND CASE SIGNS

## कारक और कारक चिह्न

*(kāraka aur kāraka chihna)*

Declension

**Masculine nouns ending in a consonant--singular**

| | | |
|---|---|---|
| नौकर ने | *naukar nē* | servant (nominative) |
| नौकर को | *naukar kō* | to the servant |
| नौकर से | *naukar sē* | from the servant |
| नौकर के लिए | *naukar kē liyē* | for the servant |
| नौकरों का, के, की | *naukar kā, kē, kī* | of the servant |

यह काम नौकर ने किया। — The servant did this work.
*yah kām naukar nē kiyā*

नौकर को काम दीजिए। — Give work to the servant.
*naukar kō kām dījiyē*

नौकर से काम लीजिए। — Take work from the servant.
*naukar sē kām lījiyē*

नौकर के लिए बहुत काम है। — There is plenty of work for the servant.
*naukar kē liyē bahut kām hai*

यह नौकर का काम है। — This is the servant's job.
*yah naukar kā kām hai*

**Plural**

| | |
|---|---|
| नौकरों ने | *ṇaukarōñ nē* |
| नौकरों को | *ṇaukarōñ kō* |
| नौकरों से | *ṇaukarōñ sē* |
| नौकरों के लिए | *ṇaukarōñ kē liyē* |
| नौकरों का, के, की | *ṇaukarōñ kā, kē, kī* |

| | |
|---|---|
| नौकरों ने काम किया । *naukarōñ nē kām kiyā* | Sẹrvants did this work. |
| नौकरों को काम दीजिए । *naukarōñ kō kām dījiyē* | Give work to the sarvants. |
| नौकरों से काम लीजिए । *naukarōñ sē kām lījiyē* | Take work from the servants. |
| नौकरों के लिए बहुत काम है । *naukarōñ kē liyē bahut kām hai* | There is plenty of work for the servants. |
| यह नौकरों का काम है । *yah naukarōñ kā kām hai* | This is the servant's job. |

**Masculine nouns ending in *ā*--singular**

| | |
|---|---|
| लड़के ने | *laḍkē nē* |
| लड़के को | *laḍkē kō* |
| लड़के से | *laḍkē sē* |
| लड़के के लिए | *laḍkē kē liyē* |
| लड़के का, के, की | *laḍkē kā, kē, kī* |

| | |
|---|---|
| लड़के ने काम किया । *laḍkē nē kām kiyā* | The boy did the work. |
| लड़के को काम दीजिए । *laḍkē kō kām dījiyē* | Give work to the boy. |
| लड़के से काम लीजिए । *laḍkē sē kām lījiyē* | Take work from the boy. |

| | |
|---|---|
| लड़के के लिए काम है। | There is work for the boy. |
| *laḍkē kē liyē kām hai* | |
| यह लड़के का काम है। | This is the boy's work. |
| *yah laḍkē dā kām hai* | |

**Plural**

| | |
|---|---|
| लड़कों ने काम किया। | The boys did the work. |
| *laḍkōñ nē kām kiyā* | |
| लड़कों को काम दीजिए। | Give work to the boys. |
| *laḍkōñ kō kām dījiyē* | |
| लड़कों से काम लीजिए। | Take work from the boys. |
| *laḍkōñ sē kām lījiyē* | |
| लड़कों के लिए काम है। | There is work for the boys. |
| *laḍkōñ kē liyē kām hai* | |
| यह काम लड़कों का है। | This is the boys' work. |
| *yah kām laḍkōñ kā hai* | |

**Masculine nouns ending in *ī* —Singular**

| | | | |
|---|---|---|---|
| आदमी ने | *ādmī nē* | आदमी के लिए | *ādmī kē liyē* |
| आदमी को | *ādmī kō* | आदमी की | *ādmī kī* |
| आदमी से | *ādmī sō* | | |

| | |
|---|---|
| आदमी ने काम किया। | The man did the work. |
| *ādmī nē kām kiyā* | |
| आदमी को काम दीजिए। | Give work to the man. |
| ādmī kō kām dījiyē | |
| आदमी से काम लीजिए। | Take work from the man. |
| *ādmī sē kām lījiyē* | |
| आदमी के लिए काम है। | There is work for the man. |
| *ādmī kē liyē kām hai* | |

| | |
|---|---|
| यह आदमी का काम है। *yah ādmī dā kām hai* | This is the man's work. |

**Masculine nouns endings in *u*—singular**

| | |
|---|---|
| गुरु ने | *guru nē* |
| गुरु को | *guru kō* |
| गुरु से | *guru sē* |
| गुरु के लिए | *guru kē liyē* |
| गुरु का | *guru kā* |

| | |
|---|---|
| गुरु ने किताब दी। *guru nē kitāb dī* | The *guru* gave the book. |
| गुरु को किताब दीजिए। *guru kō kitāb dījiyē* | Give the book to the *guru.* |
| गुरु से किताब लीजिए। *guru sē kitāb lījiyē* | Take the book from the *guru.* |
| किताब गुरु के लिए है। *kitāb guru kē liyē hai* | The book is for the *guru.* |
| किताब गुरु की है। *kitāb guru kī hai* | This is *guru's* book. |

**Plural**

| | |
|---|---|
| गुरुओं ने | *guruōñ nē* |
| गुरुओं को | *guruōñ kō* |
| गुरुओं से | *guruōñ sē* |
| गुरुओं के लिए | *guruōñ kē liyē* |
| गुरुओं की | *guruōñ kī* |

| | |
|---|---|
| गुरुओं ने किताबें दी। *guruōñ nē kitābēñ dī* | The *gurus* gave the books. |

| | |
|---|---|
| गुरुओं को किताबें दीजिए। *guruoñ kō kitābēñ dījiyē* | Give the books to the *gurus.* |
| गुरुओं से किताबें लीजिए। *guruoñ sē kitābēñ lījiyē* | Take the books from the *gurus.* |
| किताबें गुरुओं के लिए हैं। *kitābēñ guruoñ kē liyē haiñ* | The books are for the *gurus.* |

**Feminine nouns ending in ī—Singular**

| | |
|---|---|
| लड़की ने | *laḍkī nē* |
| लड़की को | *laḍkī kō* |
| लड़की से | *laḍkī sē* |
| लड़की के लिए | *laḍkī kē liyē* |
| लड़की का | *laḍkī kā* |

| | |
|---|---|
| लड़की ने माला पहनी। *laḍkī nē mālā pahani* | The girl wore the garland. |
| लड़की को माला दीजिए। *laḍkī kō mālā dījiyē* | Give the garland to the girl. |
| लड़की से माला लीजिए। ***laḍkī sē mālā lījiyē*** | Take the garland from the girl. |
| माला लड़की के लिए है। ***mālā laḍkī kē liyē hai.*** | The garland is for the girl. |
| माला लड़की की है। ***mālā laḍkī kī hai.*** | This is the girl's garland. |

**Plural**

| | |
|---|---|
| लड़कियों ने | *laḍkīyoñ nē* |
| लड़कियों को | *laḍkīyoñ kō* |
| लड़कियों से | *laḍkīyoñ sē* |

| | |
|---|---|
| लड़कियों के लिए | *laḍkīyōñ kē liyē* |
| लड़कियों का | *laḍkīyōñ kā* |

लड़कियों ने मालाएं पहनीं। — The girls wore the garlands.
*laḍkīyōñ nē mālāēñ pahani*

लड़कियों को मालाएं दीजिए। — Give the garlands to the girls.
*laḍkīyōñ kō mālāēñ dījiyē*

लड़कियों से मालाएं लीजिए। — Take the garlands from the girls.
*laḍkīyōñ sē mālāēñ lījiyē*

मालाएं लड़कियों के लिए है। — The garlands are for the girls.
*mālāēñ laḍkīyōñ kē liyē haiṇ.*

मालाएं लड़कियों की है। — There are the girl's. garlands.
*mālāēñ laḍkīyōñ kī haiṇ*

**Feminine nouns ending in a consonant--Singular**

| | |
|---|---|
| औरत ने | *aurat nē* |
| औरत को | *aurat kō* |
| औरत से | *aurat sē* |
| औरत के लिए | *aurat kē liyē* |
| औरत का | *aurat kā* |

औरत ने माला पहनी। — The woman wore the garland.
*aurat nē mālā pahani*

औरत को माला दीजिए। — Give the garland to the woman.
*aurat kō mālā dījiyē*

औरत से माला लीजिए। — Take the garland from the woman.
*aurat sē mālā lījiyē*

माला औरत के लिए है।
*mālā aurat kē liyē hai.*

The garland is for the woman.

माला औरत की है।
*mālā aurat kī hai*

The garland is the woman's.

**Rules to remember**

1. When there is a suffix to a noun which is the subject, the form of the verb changes not according to the subject, but according to the gender and number of the object, e. g., राम ने रोटी खाई *Rām nē rōṭī khāī.*
2. When there is no suffix to the noun which is the subject, the form of the verb changes according to the subject., e. g., राम रोटी खाता है *Rām rōṭī khātā hai.*
3. If a masculine noun ends in *ā,* the ending changes into *ē* when there is a suffix, e. g. लड़के को रोटी दीजिये *laḍkē kō rōṭī dījiyē.*
4. If a masculine noun ends in *ē* in the plural form, the ending changes into *ōñ* when there is a suffix to it, e.g., लड़कों को रोटी दीजिए *laḍkōñ kō rōṭī dījiyē.*
5. Feminine noun in the singular number does not change its form even when there is a suffix to it, e. g., लड़की को रोटी दीजिये *laḍkī kō rōṭī dījiyē.*
6. Feminine noun in the plural form having *yāñ* ending, changes into *yōñ* ending if there is a suffix, e.g., लड़कियों को रोटी दीजिये *laḍkīyoñ kō rōṭī dījiyē.*
7. Feminine plural nouns ending in a consonant, change into ōñ ending if there is a suffix, e. g., औरतों को रोटी दीजिये *auratōñ kō rōṭī dijiyē.*

CHAPTER FOUR

# PRONOUNS

सर्वनाम *(Sarvanām)*

**Personal Pronoun**

| | | | |
|---|---|---|---|
| First Person : | मैं | *maiñ* | I (m & f) |
| | हम | *ham* | we |
| | (Pronounced hum) | | |
| | हम लोग | *ham lōg* | we people |

(*lōg* is sometimes added to clarify the plurality)

| | | | |
|---|---|---|---|
| Second Person : | तुम | *tum* | You (m & f) |
| | तुम लोग | *tum lōg* | You people (m&f) |
| | आप | *āp* | you (m & f) |
| | आप लोग | *āp lōg* | you people (m&f) |
| Third Person : | वह | *vah* | he, she, it, that |
| | यह | *yah* | he, she, it, this |
| | वे | *vē* | they |
| | ये | *yē* | these |

In the nominative or the objective case, personal pronouns, as seen above, change only with the person or number and not with the gender.

When a pronoun is the subject, the verb takes masculine or feminine, singular or plural form accordingly as it does in the case of a noun.

| | | |
|---|---|---|
| मैं जाता हूं। | *maiñ jātā hūñ* | I go (m) |
| मैं जाती हूं। | *maiñ jāti hūñ* | I go (f) |

| | | |
|---|---|---|
| हम जाते हैं। | *ham jātē haiñ* | we go (m) |
| हम जाती हैं। | *ham jātī haiñ* | we go (f) |
| तुम जाते हो। | *tum jātē ho* | you go (m) |
| तुम जाती हो। | *tum jātī ho* | you go (f) |
| तुम लोग जाते हो। | *tum lōg jātē ho* | you people go |
| आप जाते हैं। | *āp jātē haiñ* | you go (m) |
| आप जाती हैं। | *āp jāti haiñ* | you go (f) |
| आप लोग जाते हैं। | *āp lōg jātē haiñ* | you people go. |
| वह जाता है। | *vāh jātā hai* | he goes |
| वह जाती है। | *vāh jātī hai* | she goes |
| वे जाते हैं। | *vē jātē haiñ* | they go (m) |
| वे जाती हैं। | *vē jātī haiñ* | they go (f) |

The verb *jātā* changes into *jātē,* according to the subject and is followed by the appropriate auxiliary verb.

Since the pronouns, *maiñ, tum, āp, vāh* etc. are common for feminine and masculine the verb indicates whether the subject is masculine or feminine.

There two forms of personal pronoun in the second person -*tum* and *ap.* Usually *tum* is used for a person who is either very familiar or much younger in age. It is also often used for a person much below in social status. *āp* is the respectful form of address. It is also formal and used for people with whom one is not so familiar. Since one is likely to commit mistakes which may sound impolite, it is better always to use *āp.*

There is yet another form *tū,* (thou) which is either very familiar, and an expression of endearment, or it is derogatory, depending on for whom it is used. God is sometimes addressed as *tū.* Its equivalent in English would be thou. It is better not to use *tū.* to avoid using it in wrong places and for the wrong person.

**Possessive Pronouns**

Possessive pronouns differ with the first, second and third person. They decline according to the noun they qualify. For example, my brother would be *mērā bhāī* and my sister would be *mēri bahin,* whether a man speaks or a woman. Similarly in the third person *his dog* or *her dog* would both be *uskā kuttā,* since *kuttā* is masculine; *his mother* or *her mother* would both be *uski mā,* since *mañ* is feminine. The first important step would be to learn the possessive pronouns by heart.

| | | |
|---|---|---|
| मेरा, मेरी, मेरे | *mērā, mērī, mērē* | my, mine |
| हमारा, हमारी, हमारे | *hamārā, hamārī, hamārē* | our, ours |
| तुम्हारा, तुम्हारी, तुम्हारे | *tumhārā, tumhārī, tumhārē* | your, yours |
| आपका, आपकी, आपके | *āpakā, āpakī, āpakē* | your, yours |
| उसका, उसकी, उसके | *uskā, usakī, usakē* | his or hers |
| उनका, उनकी, उनके | *unkā, unkī, unkē* | their, theirs |

**Case**

*Suffixes or Case-signs*

| | | |
|---|---|---|
| ने | *nē* | nominative-case in present perfect and past perfect |
| को | *kō* | to |
| से | *sē* | with, from |
| के द्वारा | *kē dvārā* | by, through |
| के लिए | *kē liyē* | for |

| | | |
|---|---|---|
| का, की, के | *kā, kī, kē* | of |
| में | *mēñ* | in, inside |
| पर | *par* | on, upon |

When suffixed to personal pronouns :

First Person :

| | | |
|---|---|---|
| मैं | *maiñ* | I |
| मैंने | *maiñē* | I (nominative case in present perfect and past perfect) |
| मेरा | *mērā* | my, mine |
| मुझको | *mujhkō* | to me |
| मुझसे | *mujhsē* | to me, from me, with me |
| मुझसे | *mujhsē* | by me, |
| मेरे द्वारा | *mērē dvārā* | through me |
| मेरे लिए | *mērē liyē* | for me |
| मुझमें | *mujhmē* | in me |
| मुझ पर | *mujh par* | on me |

Second Person :

| | | |
|---|---|---|
| तुम | *tum* | you |
| तुमने | *tumnē* | you (nominative) |
| तुम्हारा | *tumhārā* | your, yours |
| तुमको | *tumkō* | to you |
| तुमसे | *tumse* | from you |
| तुम्हारे द्वारा | *tumharē dvāra* | by you, through you |
| तुमसे | *tumsē* | |
| तुम्हारे लिए | *tumharē liyē* | for you |
| तुम में | *tum mēñ* | in you |
| तुम पर | *tum par* | on you |

| | | |
|---|---|---|
| आप | *āp* | you |
| आपने | *āpnē* | you (nominative) |
| आपका | *āpkā* | of you, yours |
| आपको | *āpkā* | to you |
| आपसे | *āpsē* | from you |
| आपसे, आपके द्वारा | *āpsē, āpkē dvāra* | by you, through you |
| आपके लिए | *āpkē liyē* | for you. |
| आपमें, आप पर | *āpmēñ, āp par* | in you, on you |

Third Person :

| | | |
|---|---|---|
| वह | *vah* | he, she, it, that, |
| उसने | *usnē* | he, she, it (nominative) |
| उसका | *uskā* | his, her's, its |
| उसको | *uskō* | to him, to her, to it |
| उससे | *ussē* | from him, from her, from it |
| उसके द्वारा | *uskē dvārā* | by him/her/it |
| उसके लिए | *uskē liyē* | for him/her/it |
| उसमें, उस पर | *usmē, us par* | in him, on him/her/it |
| वे | *vē* | they |
| उन्होंने | *unhōnē* | they (nominative) |
| उनका | *unkā* | their, theirs |
| उनको | *unkō* | to them |
| उनसे | *unsē* | from them |
| उनसे | *unsē,* | by them, |
| उनके द्वारा | *unkē dvārā* | through them |
| उनके लिए | *unkē liyē* | for them |
| उनमें, उन पर | *unmēñ, un par* | in them, on them |

**Examples**

First Person :

| | | |
|---|---|---|
| मैंने रोटी खाई । | *maiñ nē roṭī khāyī* | I ate bread. |
| यह मेरा घर है । | *yah mērā ghar hai* | This is my house. |
| किताब मुझको दीजिए । | *kitāb mujhkō dījiyē* | Give the book to me. |
| मुझसे यह काम नहीं होगा । | *mujhsē yah kām nahīñ hōgā* | This work cannot be done by me. |
| आप मेरे लिए क्या लाए हैं ? | *āp mērē liyē kyā lāyē haiñ ?* | What have you brought for me ? |
| मुझसे आपको क्या चाहिए ? | *mujhsē āpkō kyā chāhiyē ?* | What do you want from me ? |
| मेरी बेटी घर में है । | *mērī bēṭī ghar mēñ hai* | My daughter is in the house. |
| मुझ पर दया कीजिए | *mujh par dayā kījiyē* | Have pity on me. |

Second Person :

| | | |
|---|---|---|
| * तुमने रोटी खाई ? | *tumnē rōṭī khāyī ?* | Have you had your meal ? |
| तुम्हारा घर कहां है ? | *tumhārā ghar kahāñ hai ?* | Where is you house? |
| तुमको पत्र किसने दिया ? | *tūmkō patra kisnē diyā ?* | Who gave you the letter ? |
| वह तुमसे कितने रुपए मांगता है ? | *vah tumsē kitanē rupayē māñgtā hai ?* | How many rupees is the asking from you ? |

* In north India when a person speaks of eating *rōṭī* he often means eating a meal.

| | | |
|---|---|---|
| तुमसे उसका काम हो सकेगा ? | *tumse uskā kām hō sakēgā ?* | Can his work be done by you ? |
| वह तुम्हारे लिए क्या लाया है ? | *vah tūmhārē liyē kyā lāyā hai ?* | What has he brought for you ? |
| उसको तुम पर भरोसा है ? | *uskō tum par bharōsā hai ?* | Does he trust you ? |
| आपने क्या कहा ? | *āpnē kyā kahā ?* | What did you say ? |
| आपका शुभ नाम क्या है ? | *āpakā shubh nām kyā hai ?* | What is you name ? |

(It is not ver polite to ask *āpkā nām kyā hai* ? Many Indians wrongly translate this literally into English as: What is your good name ?)

| | | |
|---|---|---|
| आपको क्या चाहिए ? | *āpkō kyā chāhiyē ?* | What do you want ? |
| मुझको आपसे एक किताब चाहिए। | *mujhkō ākpsē ēk kitāb chāhiyē* | I want a book from you. |
| आपसे यह काम होगा ? | *āpasē yah kām hōgā ?* | Can this work be done by you ? |
| मैं आपके लिए फूल लायी हूं। | *main āpkē līyē phūl lāyī hūñ* | I have brought flowers for you. |
| आपमें बहुत गुण हैं। | *āpmēñ bahut guṇ haiñ* | You have many good qualities. |
| मुझको आप पर भरोसा है। | *mujh kō āp par bharōsā hai* | I trust you. |

Third Person :

| | | |
|---|---|---|
| उसने क्या कहा था ? | *usnē kyā kahā thā ?* | What did he say ? |

| | | |
|---|---|---|
| उसका घर कहां है ? | *uskā ghar kahāñ hai ?* | Where is his house ? |
| उसको क्या चाहिए ? | *uskō kyā chāhiyē ?* | What does he want ? |
| उससे रुपए मांगो । | *mssē rupayē māñgō* | Ask him for money. |
| उससे यह काम नहीं हो सकता । | *ussē yah kām nāhiñ hō saktā* | This work cannot be done by him. |
| मैं उसके लिए खाना लाता हूं । | *maiñ uskē līyē khānā lātā hūñ* | I bring food for him. |
| मेरे कपड़े उसमें नहीं है । | *mērē kapḍē usmēñ nahiñ haiñ* | My clothes are not in that. |
| इस पर किताबें मत रखो । | *is par kitābēñ mat rakhō* | Don't keep the books on this. |

In the case of the third person the pronouns *us* or *is* may be used to qualify a noun, e. g., *on that table--us mēz par;* in this cupboard--*is almarī meñ.* As prepositions are actually postpositions in Hindi, they are placed *after and not before* a noun or a pronoun.

**More Examples :**

| | | |
|---|---|---|
| मेरी किताबें उस अलमारी में हैं । | *mērī kitābēñ us almārī mēñ haiñ* | My books are in that cupboard. |
| राम इस घर में रहता है । | *Rām is ghar mēñ rahtā hai* | Ram lives in this house. |
| सीता उस स्कूल में पढ़ाती है । | *Sita us skūl mēñ paḍhātī hai* | Sita teaches in that school. |
| प्याले उस मेज़ पर रखो । | *payālē us mēz par rākhō* | Put the cups on that table. |

| | | |
|---|---|---|
| उस कमरे को साफ करो । | *us kamare kō sāf karō* | Clean that room. |
| रुपए उस जेब में हैं । | *rupayē us jēb mēñ haiñ* | Money is in that pocket. |

**New Words :**

| | | | |
|---|---|---|---|
| *tākat* | strength | *dayā* | pity |
| *kījiyē* | please do | *patra* | letter |
| *māñgtā* | asks for | *lāyā* | has brought |
| *bharōsā* | trust | *shubh* | auspicious, good |
| *guṇ* | virtues | *almārī* | cupboard |
| *paḍhātī* | teaches | *jēb* | pocket |

CHAPTER FIVE

# PREPOSITIONS

## विभक्ति-चिह्न *(Vibhakti Chihna)*

A preposition, as already explained, is actually a post-position in Hindi as it occurs not *before* but *after* a noun or pronoun. For example, *on the table* would be *table on* and *in the room* would be *room in. The book is on the table* would be *the book table on is (kitāb mēz par hai)*

**Post-positions or case-signs**

| | | |
|---|---|---|
| ने | *nē* | (nominative case present perfect and past perfect) |
| का, की, के | *kā, kī, kē* | of |
| को | *kō* | to |
| से | *sē* | from, with and by |
| पर | *par* | on, above |
| में | *mēñ* | in |

Prepositions in Hindi are suffixes to *pronouns, but* they are written as separate words with nouns.

**Examples :**

| | | | |
|---|---|---|---|
| *Rām kō* | but | *mujhkō* | (to me) |
| *mēz par* | but | *uspar* | (on that) |
| *kamarē mēñ* | but | *usmēñ* | (in that) |
| *Rām nē* | but | *mainē* | (I) |

*Kē sāth* is also used to mean together with or in the company of.

For example, *I shall go with you* would be *maiñ āpkē sāth jāūñgā.* But *I write with a pen* would be *maiñ kalam sē likhatā hūñ. I wash clothes with soap* would be *maiñ sabun sē kapḍē dhōtā hūñ.*

**Further examples :**

He eats with a spoon--*Vah chammach sē khātā hai.*

He cuts the mango with the knife--*Vah chhurī sē ām kaṭatā hai.*

When a noun is not followed by a post-position or a case sign, it changes from singular to plural as already explained in detail in the chapter on nouns. But if it is followed by a post position, it changes by adding *ē* to the masculine singular, and *ōñ* to masculine plural. In the case of feminine nouns, there is no change in the case of singular but *āñ* is added in the end for plural. Examples :

**Without post-position :**

| Singular | | Plural | |
|---|---|---|---|
| कमरा | *kamarā* (m) | कमरे | *kamarē* |
| कुरसी | *kursī* (f) | कुरसियाँ | *kursiyāñ* |

**With post-position**

| Singular | | Plural | |
|---|---|---|---|
| कमरे में | *kamarē mēñ* | कमरों में | *kamarōñ mēñ* |
| कुरसी पर | *kursī par* | कुरसियों पर | *kursiōñ par* |

**Examples :**

| | | |
|---|---|---|
| कमरा साफ है। | *kamarā sāf hai* | The room is clean. |
| कमरे साफ हैं। | *kamarē sāf haiñ* | The rooms are clean. |

| | | |
|---|---|---|
| कमरे में गरमी है। | *kamarē mēñ garmī hai* | It is hot in the room. |
| कमरों में गरमी है। | *kamarōñ mēñ garmī hai* | It is hot in the rooms. |
| घर में जाले हैं। | *ghar mēñ jālē haiñ* | There are cobwebs in the house. |
| घरों में जाले हैं। | *gharōñ mēñ jālē haiñ* | There are cobwebs in the houses. |

**Other Examples** (Feminine nouns)

| | | |
|---|---|---|
| मेज़ पर किताब है। | *mēz par kitāb hai* | The book is on the table. |
| मेज़ों पर किताबें है। | *mēzoñ par kitābēñ haiñ* | Books are on the tables. |
| कुरसी पर धूल है। | *kursī par dhūl hai* | There is dust on the chair. |
| कुरसियों पर धूल है। | *kursīyōñ par dhūl hai* | There is dust on the chairs. |

**Reading Exercise :**

| | | |
|---|---|---|
| छोटा चम्मच प्याले में है। | *chhōṭạ chammach pyālē mēñ hai* | The small spoon is in the cup. |
| प्यालों में चम्मच नहीं हैं। | *pyāloñ mēñ chammach nahiñ haiñ* | There are no spoons in the cups. |
| मेरा कुत्ता बीमार है। | *mērā kuttā bīmār hai* | My dog is sick. |

| | | |
|---|---|---|
| कुत्ते को डाक्टर के पास ले जाइए। | *kuttē kō dōcṭar kē pās lē jāiyē* | Please take the dog to the doctor. |
| कुत्ते के लिए दवा लाइए। | *kuttē kē liyē davā lāiyē* | Please bring a medicine for the dog. |
| अपने कुत्तों को यहां मत लाइए। | *apnē kuttōñ kō yahāñ mat lāiyē* | Please dont bring your dogs here. |
| सड़क पर बहुत पानी है। | *saḍak par bahut pānī hai* | There is a lot of water on the road. |
| सड़कों पर बहुत पानी है। | *saḍkōñ par bahut pānī hai* | There is a lot of water on the roads. |
| * इस शीशे को साफ़ करो। | *is shīshē kō sāf karō* | Clean this mirror. |
| इन शीशों को साफ़ करो। | *in shīshōñ kō sāf karō* | Clean this mirrors. |

* This can be said without the post-position--*vah shīshā sāf karō*. But when the post-position *kō* is used *shīshā* becomes *shīshē*.

CHAPTER SIX

# ADJECTIVES

## विशेषण *(Vishēṣhaṇ)*

| | | |
|---|---|---|
| यह गोरा लड़का है। | *yah gōrā laḍkā hai* | This boy is fair. |
| ये गोरे लड़के हैं। | *yē gōrē laḍkē haiñ* | These boys are fair. |
| यह गोरी लड़की है। | *yah gōrī laḍki hai* | This girl is fair. |
| ये गोरी लड़कियाँ | *yē gōrī laḍkiyāñ* | These girls are fair. |
| यह बड़ा घर है। | *yah baḍā ghar hai* | This is a big house. |
| ये बड़े घर हैं। | *yē bāḍē ghar haiñ* | These are big houses. |
| यह बड़ी मेज है। | *yah baḍi mēz hai* | This is a big table. |
| ये बड़ी मेज़ें हैं। | *yē baḍi mēzēñ haiñ* | These are big tables. |

1. If an adjective ends with *ā* sound, it declines according to the number and gender of the noun it qualifies. In the first set of sentences above, the noun *laḍkā* and the qualifying adjective *gōrā* both have *ā* ending and decline. But it would also be noticed that in the case of feminine plural, the adjective does not change its form, e.g. *laḍkiyāñ gōrī haiñ.*

2. In the second set of sentences, while the adjective *baḍa* ends in *ā,* the nouns *ghar* and *mēz* end in a consonant. But the adjecitve declines as it does in the first set of sentences. The second rule to remember, therefore, is : *an adjective ending in ā sound will change its ending according to the number*

*and gender of the noun it qualifies even if the noun does not end in ā sound.* Some more examples would clarify the point further.

| | | |
|---|---|---|
| मीठा केला | *mīṭhā kēlā* | sweet banana |
| मीठे केले | *mīṭhē kēlē* | sweet bananas |
| मीठी नारंगी | *mīṭhī nārangī* | sweet tangarine |
| मीठी नारंगियां | *mīṭhī nārangiāñ* | sweet tangarines |
| मोटा आदमी | *mōṭā ādmī* | fat man |
| मोटे आदमी | *mōṭē ādmī* | fat men |
| मोटी औरत | *mōṭī aurat* | fat woman |
| मोटी औरतें | *mōṭī auratēñ* | fat women |
| अच्छा शहर | *achchhā shahar* | good city |
| अच्छे शहर | *achchhē shahar* | good cities |
| अच्छी जगह | *achchhī jagah* | good place |
| अच्छी जगहें | *achchhī jaghēñ* | good places |

In the examples given above the nouns *shahar* and *jagah* have consonant endings, but the adjectives decline since they end in *ā*.

3. If the adjective does not end with *ā*, it *never* changes its form. Examples :

| | | |
|---|---|---|
| वीर लड़का | *vīr laḍkā* | brave boy |
| वीर लड़के | *vīr laḍkē* | brave boys |
| वीर लड़की | *vīr laḍkī* | brave girl |
| वीर लड़कियां | *vīr laḍkiyāñ* | brave girls |
| गरम पकौड़ा | *garam pakauḍā* | hot *pakaura* |
| गरम पकौड़े | *garam pakauḍē* | hot *pakauras* |
| गरम रोटी | *garam rōṭī* | hot *roti* |
| गरम रोटियां | *garam rōṭiyāñ* | hot *rotis* |

4. There are some other rules of usage which should be remembered.

(a) Words indicating the profession of a person have a masculine gender even if the last syllable of the word is *ī* e. g., *mālī* (gardener); *nāī* (barber); *kasāī* (butcher); *dhobī* (washerman).

(b) Names of rivers are always of the feminine gender.

(c) Names of the days of the week are of masculine gender.

(d) Certain birds and animals such as *kōyal* (cuckoo), *battakh* (duck), *gilahrī* (squirrel), *lomṛi* (fox) are always used in the feminine gender.

(e) Certain other animals such as *bhēḍiyā* (wolf), *chītā* (cheetah), *tēnduā* (leopard) are always used in the masculine gender.

5. Sometimes when the subject is in the plural, the adjective is repeated for emphasis and good expression, e. g.,

| | | |
|---|---|---|
| सुन्दर-सुन्दर फूल | *sundar-sundar phūl* | beautiful flowers |
| बड़े-बड़े मकान | *baḍē-baḍē makān* | big houses |
| गरम-गरम रोटियां | *garam-garam rōṭiyāñ* | hot bread |
| मीठे-मीठे फल | *mīṭhē-mīṭhē phal* | sweet fruits |

6. There are some adjectives which do not change form with change in number or gender. For example.

| | | |
|---|---|---|
| अमीर | *amīr* | rich |
| गरीब | *garīb* | poor |
| जवान | *jawān* | young |

| | | |
|---|---|---|
| खराब | *kharāb* | bad, poor in quality |
| खूबसूरत | *khūbsūrat* | beautiful |
| बढ़िया | *baḍhiyā* | excellent, of high quality |
| ईमानदार | *īmāndār* | honest |
| बेईमान | *bēīmān* | dishonest |
| सुस्त | *sust* | dull |
| तेज़ | *tēz* | sharp, fast |
| चालाक | *chālāk* | cunning |

7. These adjectives are originally derived from Urdu adopted in Hindi like hundred of other Urdu words and are a part of the spoken Hindi now.

Let us use them in sentences.

| | | |
|---|---|---|
| यह आदमी अमीर है। | *yah ādmaī amīr hai* | This man is rich. |
| यह औरत अमीर है। | *yah aurat amīr hai* | This woman is rich. |
| ये लोग गरीब हैं। | *yē lōg garīb haiñ* | These people are poor. |
| मैं गरीब हूं। | *maiñ garīb hūñ* | I am poor. |
| यह लड़का जवान है। | *yah laḍkā jawān hai* | This boy is young. |
| ये लड़कियां जवान हैं। | *yē laḍkiyāñ jawān haiñ* | These girls are young. |
| यह शहर खूबसूरत है। | *yah shahar khūbsūrat hai* | This city is beautiful. |
| ये फूल खूबसूरत हैं। | *yē phūl khūsbsūrat haiñ* | These flowers are beautiful. |
| मेरा माली ईमानदार है। | *mērā mālī īmāndār hai* | My gardener is honest. |

| | | |
|---|---|---|
| मेरा दूधवाला बेईमान है। | *mērā dūdhvālā bēīmān hai* | My milkman is dishonest. |
| यह छुरी तेज़ है। | *yah chhurī tēz hai* | This knife is sharp. |
| ये छुरियाँ तेज़ हैं। | *yē chhuriyāñ tēz haiñ* | These knives are sharp. |

8. The comparative and superlative degrees of an adjective are indicated by adding words to the positive adjective, for example :

| Positive | Comparative | Superlative |
|---|---|---|
| *achchhā* (good) | *ussē achchhā* (better) | *sabsē achchhā* (best) |
| *kharāb* (bad) | *ussē kharāb* (worse) | *sabsē kharāb* (worst) |
| *sundar* (pretty) | *ussē sundar* (prettier) | *sabsē sunder* (prettiest) |

The examples given for the comparative degree mean better than that, worse than that, or prettier than that. More concrete comparisons would be :

| | | |
|---|---|---|
| राम अच्छा लड़का है। | *Rām achchhā laḍkā hai* | Ram is a good boy. |
| श्याम राम से अच्छा है। | *Shyām Rām sē achchhā hai* | Shyam is better than Ram. |
| हरी सबसे अच्छा लड़का है। | *Harī sabsē achchhā laḍkā hai* | Hari is the best boy. |
| कलकत्ता भारत का सबसे बड़ा शहर है। | *Kalkattā Bhārat kā sabsē baḍā shahar hai* | Calcutta is the biggest city of India. |

(Literally *sabsē baḍā* means, bigger than all.)

| | | |
|---|---|---|
| गुलाब सबसे सुन्दर फूल है। | *Gulāb sabsē sundar phūl hai* | Rose is the prettiest flower. |
| राम श्याम से ज्यादा होशियार है। | *Rām Shyām sē zyādā hōshiyār hai* | Ram is more intelligent than Shyam. |
| कक्षा में राम सबसे ज़्यादा होशियार है | *kakshā mēñ Rām sabsē zyādā hōshiyār hai* | Ram is most intelligent in the class. |

Sometimes superlatives are also expressed in the following manner :

| | | |
|---|---|---|
| अच्छे से अच्छा | *achchhē sē achchhā* | best |
| खराब से खराब | *kharāb sē kharāb* | worst |
| मज़बूत से मज़बूत | *mazbūt sē mazbūt* | strongest |
| कमज़ोर से कमज़ोर | *kamzōr sē kamzōr* | weakest |

(Literally, these read—better than good; worse than bad; stronger than strong; weaker than weak.)

**Adjectives in pairs**

Two adjecitves similar in meaning are used as one phrase for emphasis and colourful expression. For example :

| | | |
|---|---|---|
| साफ-सुथरा | *sāf-suthrā* | neat and clean |
| मैला-कुचैला | *mailā-kuchailā* | very filthy |

(The word *kuchailā* is never used by itself.)

| | | |
|---|---|---|
| सड़ा-गला | *saḍā-galā* | rotten |
| आपका घर कितना साफ-सुथरा है। | *āpkā ghar kitnā sāf-suthrā hai* | How clean is your house ! |

Some more examples :

| | | |
|---|---|---|
| मेरा काला कोट कहां है ? | *mērā kālā kōṭ kahāñ hai ?* | Where is my black coat ? |
| यह कोट तो मैला है। | *yah kōṭ ṭō mailā hai* | This coat is dirty. |
| यह धोबी अच्छा नहीं है। | *yah dhōbī achchhā nahīñ hai* | This washerman is not good. |
| यह रोटी बिल्कुल ठंडी है। | *yah rōṭī bilkul ṭhanḍī hai* | This roti is absolutely cold. |
| गरम रोटी लाइए। | *garam rōṭī lāiyē* | Please bring hot roti. |
| ये आम बिल्कुल खट्टे हैं। | *yē ām bilkul khaṭṭē haiñ* | These mangoes are absolutely sour. |
| मीठे-मीठे आम लाइए। | *mīṭhē-mīṭhē- ām lāiyē* | Please bring sweet mangoes. |
| आपकी यह आदत बहुत बुरी है। | *āpkī yah ādat bahut burī hai* | This habit of yours is very bad. |
| बच्चों की आदतें अच्छी नहीं हैं। | *bachchōñ kī adatēñ achchhī nahīñ haiñ* | Childern's habits are not good. |
| आपकी हरी साड़ी सुन्दर है। | *apkī harī sāṛī sundar hai* | Your green sari is pretty. |
| क्या बहुत महंगी है ? | *kyā bahut mahagī hai ?* | Is it very expensive ? |
| जी नहीं, बहुत महंगी नहीं है। | *jī nahīñ bahut mahañgi nahīñ hai* | No, it is not very expensive. |
| आज कमरा साफ़ नहीं है। | *āj kamarā sāf nahīñ hai* | Today the room is not clean. |

| | | |
|---|---|---|
| जमादार बहुत सुस्त है । | *jamādār bahut sust hai* | The sweeper is very lazy. |
| वह बेचारा बीमार है । | *vah bĕchārā bīmār hai* | The poor fellow is sick. |
| वह बहुत लापरवाह है । | *vah bahut lāparvāh hai* | He is very careless. |
| उसके बच्चे बहुत दुबले-पतले हैं । | *uskē bachchē bahut dublē-patlē haiñ* | His children are very lean and thin. |
| वे कमजोर हैं | *vē kamzōr hain* | They are weak |
| क्योंकि काफी दूध नहीं पीते । | *kyōnki kāfi dūdh nahīñ pītē* | because they don't drink enough milk. |
| यह दुकान बहुत महंगी है । | *yah dukān bahut mahañgi hai* | This shop is very expensive. |
| दूसरी दुकान कम महंगी है । | *dūsarī dukān kam mahañgi hai* | The other shop is less expensive. |
| वह दुकानदार ईमानदार है । | *vah dukānkar īmāndār hai* | That shopkeeper is honest. |

**New words in this chapter**

| | | |
|---|---|---|
| मैला | *mailā* | dirty |
| धोबी | *dhōbī* | washerman |
| बिल्कुल | *bilkul* | absolutely |
| ठंडी | *ṭhanḍi* | cold |
| लाइए | *lāiyē* | please bring |
| खट्टा | *khaṭṭā* | sour |
| आदत | *ādat* | habit |
| हरी | *harī* | green |

| | | |
|---|---|---|
| महंगी | *mahañgī* | expensive |
| साफ़ | *sāf* | clean |
| सुस्त | *sust* | lazy, inactive, slow |
| काफ़ी | *kāfī* | enough, sufficient |
| पीते | *pītē* | drink |
| दुकान | *dūkān* | shop |
| | | |
| कम | **kam* | less |
| मीठे-मीठे | *mīṭhē-mīṭhē* | sweet |
| लापरवाह | *lāparvāh* | careless |
| दुबले-पतले | *dublē-patlē* | lean and thin |
| दुकानदार | *dūkāndār* | shopkeeper |

* कम *kam* should not be confused with काम *kām*. The former means less and the latter means work. So *kam kām* would mean less work.

CHAPTER SEVEN

# VERBS

## क्रिया *(Kriyā)*

The verb is the most important part of a sentence. If you have mastered the verb, you have mastered the language. Here we shall explain the basic forms of the verb without giving the tongue-twisting names of its various forms.

As in English, there are three tenses *(kāl)* in Hindi too. Present, Future and Past--*vartamān, bhavishya, bhūt.*

The auxiliary verbs, which have already been introduced in the chapter on pronouns, are given here again for not only refreshing your memory but for memorising them.

These are extremely important.

| | | |
|---|---|---|
| हूं | *hūñ* | am |
| है | *hai* | is |
| हैं | *haiñ* | are |
| था, थी | *thā, thī* | was |
| थे, थीं | *thē, thiñ* | were |
| गा, गी, गे | *gā, gī, gē* | will, shall |

As already explained earlier, the *verb always comes last in a sentence and the auxiliary verb comes at the very end. In an interrogative sentence the verb does not change its place.* The interrogation is indicated by the tone of the speech. For example :

आपका नाम राम है। Your name is Ram.

*āpkā nām Rām hai.*

आपका नाम राम है। Your name is Ram ?

*āpkā nām Rām hai ?*

Sometimes a question may be emphasised by adding *kyā* (what) at the beginning.

क्या आपका नाम राम है। Is your name Ram ?

*kyā āpkā nām Rām hai ?*

Present Indefinite Tense

| | | |
|---|---|---|
| मैं जाता हूं। | *maiñ jātā hūñ* | I go (m) |
| मैं जाती हूं। | *maiñ jātī hūñ* | I go (f) |
| हम जाते हैं। | *hum jātē haiñ* | We go |
| तुम जाते हो। | *tum jātē hō* | You go (m) |
| तुम जाती हो। | *tum jātī hō* | You go (f) |
| आप जाते हैं। | *āp jātē haiñ* | You go (m) |
| आप जाती हैं। | *āp jātī haiñ* | You go (f) |
| वह जाता है। | *vah jātā hai* | He goes |
| वह जाती है। | *vah jātī hai* | She goes |
| वे जाते है। | *vē jātē haiñ* | They go (m) |
| वे जाती हैं। | *vē jātī haiñ* | They go (f) |

The sentences given earlier are in the present indefinite tense. It is formed by adding *tā, tī,* or *tē* to the stem of the verb, depending on the gender and the number of the subject, and adding the proper auxiliary verb in the end. For example, take the first sentence. The stem of the verb *jātā* is *jā.* if the subject is mascûline singular, *tā* is added to stem making it *jātā.* Similarly in the second sentence *tī* has been added to *jā* making it *jātī* as the subject is feminine. The form of the verb, therefore, depends not only on the tense and mood but also on the subject.

Let us take another verb, *pīnā* (to drink), We shall first take nouns as subjects and then pronouns.

| | |
|---|---|
| *Rām kyā pītā hai ?* | What does Ram drink ? |
| *Rām dūdh pītā hai ?* | Ram drinks milk ? |
| *Sītā kyā pītī hai ?* | What does Sita drink ? |
| *Sītā pānī pītī hai ?* | Sita drinks water. |
| *jī hañ, Rām aur Sītā chāe pītē haiñ* | Yes, Ram and Sita drink tea. |
| *Rām aur Sītā chāe nahīñ pītē, dūdh pītē haiñ* | Ram and Sita do not drink tea, they drink milk. |

Several points can be noticed in the above sentences.

1. Since the verb *pīnā is* transitive, there is an object in every sentence which does not affect the verb.
2. The verb is still governed by the subject, whether noun or pronoun.
3. The sentence *'jī hāñ, Rām aur Sītā chāe pītē haiñ'* has two subjects, one masculine, the other feminine. In such cases, the verb will be masculine plural.
4. The last sentence is a compound sentence.

The first sentence is negative, *Rāṃ aur Sītā chāe nahīñ pītē haiñ. jī hāñ* (yes) is added for emphasis and clarity. *jī* is added for politeness and is like saying 'Yes, please.'

Now, if the subject is a pronoun :

| | |
|---|---|
| *maiñ khātā hūñ* | I eat. |
| *maiñ khātī hūñ* | I eat. (f) |
| *ham khātē haiñ* | We eat. |

| | |
|---|---|
| *tum khātē hō* | You eat. |
| *tum khātī hō* | You eat.(f) |
| *tum lōg khātī hō* | You (people) eat. (f) |
| *āp khātē haiñ* | You eat. |
| *āp khātī haiñ* | You eat. (f) |
| *āp lōg khātē haiñ* | You (people) eat. |
| *vah khātā hai* | He eats. |
| *vah khāti hai* | She eats. |
| *vē khātē haiñ* | They eat. |
| *vē khātī haiñ* | They eat. (f) |

It is advisable to read aloud this table to understand clearly and to memorize the rules by which the form of a verb is changed. A list of verbs of common usage is given at the end of the book. The reader is advised to take a few words and form sentences based on the examples given here. But the most important thing is to use what you learn. If you commit mistakes, which you will, in the early stages, they will get corrected in the process and you will be able to express yourself clearly and confidently.

**Present Continuous**

| | | |
|---|---|---|
| मैं जा रहा हूं। | *maiñ jā rahā hūñ* | I am going. (m) |
| मैं जा रही हूं। | *maiñ jā rahī hūñ* | I am going. (f) |
| हम जा रहे हैं। | *ham jā rahē haiñ* | We are going. |
| तुम जा रहे हो। | *tum jā rahē hō* | You are going. (m) |
| तुम जा रही हो। | *tum jā rahī hō* | You are going. (f) |
| आप जा रहे हैं। | *āp jā rahē haiñ* | You are going. (m) |
| आप जा रही हैं। | *āp jā rahī haiñ* | You are going. (f) |
| आप लोग जा रहे हैं। | *āp lōg jā rahē haiñ* | You (people) are going. |

| | | |
|---|---|---|
| वह जा रहा है। | *vah jā rahā hai* | He is going. |
| वे जा रहे हैं। | *vē jā rahē haiñ* | They are going. (m) |
| वे जा रही हैं। | *vē jā rahī haiñ* | They are going. (f) |

Although the familiar and informal form of address, *tum,* has been given throughout this book, it is better to use only *āp* as far as possible, not only to make learning simpler and easier, but also to avoid any possible embarrassment, for, unless you are very familiar with the perosn, or he or she is much younger to you, *tum* may sound impolite and disrespectful.

Even when referring to a third person who is not present, it would be advisable to use the verb in the third person plural to show respect. For instance, if you are referring to the President of India *(Rāshṭrapati)* it would be very impolite and discourteous to say *Rāshṭrapati ā rahā hai.* The proper form would be *Rashṭrapati ā rahē haiñ*

*The point to remember is that the plural form of a verb, when the subject is second or third person, is the polite form and, therefore, safer to use.*

Similarly, if you are referring to someone's parents, husband or wife, courtesy demands that you use the plural form of the verb. For example :

| | |
|---|---|
| *āpkē patī kaisē haiñ* ? | How is your husband ? |
| *āpkī patnī kaisī haiñ ?* | How is your wife ? |

and not *āpkā patī kaisā hai* or *āpkī patnī kaisī hai.*

Please also note that the possessive pronoun *āpkā* also takes the plural form *āpkē* in concord with the plural form of the verb.

**Present Perfect**

When a job has been completed now or in the very near past, the verb is in the present perfect. But in this form there is a variation in the rules regarding transitive verbs and intransitive verbs. We shall first take an example of an intransitive verb--*ānā* (to come).

To get the present perfect form *ā, ā-ī, ā-ē,* is added to the stem of the principal verb which is followed by the auxiliary verb.

| | | |
|---|---|---|
| मैं आया हूं। | *maiñ āyā hūñ* | I have come. |
| मैं आयी हूं। | *maiñ āyī hūñ* | I have come. (f) |
| हम आये हैं। | *hum āyā haiñ* | We have come. (f & m) |
| तुम आये हो। | *tum āyē hō* | You have come. |
| तुम आयी हो। | *tum āyī hō* | You have come. (f) |
| आप आये हैं। | *āp āyē haiñ* | You have come. |
| आप आयी हैं। | *āp āyī haiñ* | You have come. (f) |
| आप लोग आये हैं। | *āp lōg āyē haiñ* | You (people) have come. |
| वह आया है। | *vah āyā hai* | He has come. |
| वह आयी है। | *vah āyī hai* | She has come. |
| वह आये हैं। | *vah āyē haiñ* | They have come. |
| वह आयी है। | *vē āyī haiñ* | They have come. |

When the verb is transitive, *nē* is added as a suffix to the subject--noun or pronoun. Study the sentences given as examples and read them aloud several times.

| | | |
|---|---|---|
| मैंने खाया है। | *mainē khāyā hai* | I have eaten. |
| हमने खाया है | *hamnē khāyā hai* | We have eaten. |
| तुमने खाया है। | *tumnē khāyā hai* | You have eaten. |
| आपने खाया है। | *apnē khāyā hai* | You have eaten. |
| उसने खाया है। | *usnē khāyā hai* | He/she has eaten. |
| उन्होंने खाया है। | *unhōnē khāyā hai* | They have eaten. |

The verbs, both the principal and the auxiliary, have not changed with the person, number or gender even though the object has not been mentioned.

When the object is not mentioned, the transitive verb is always in the masculine singular form.

**More examples :**

| | | |
|---|---|---|
| मैंने पिया है। | *mainē piyā hai* | I have drunk. |
| हमने पिया है। | *hamnē piyā hai* | We have drunk. |
| तुमने पिया है। | *tumnē piyā hai* | You have drunk. |
| उसने पिया है। | *usnē piyā hai* | He/She have drunk. |
| उन्होंने पिया है। | *unhōnē piyā hai* | They have drunk. |

The important points to remember in the case of the present prefect are :

(i) **ने (*nē*) is added as a suffix to the subject--noun or pronoun.**

(ii) **the verb does not change with the subject.**

(iii) **the verb changes with the object.**

| | | |
|---|---|---|
| मैंने रोटी खायी। | *mainē rōṭī khāyī* | I ate bread. |
| आपने रोटियां खायीं। | *āpnē rōṭiyāñ khāyiñ* | You ate bread. |
| मैंने केला खाया। | *mainē kēlā khāyā* | I ate a banana. |

| | | |
|---|---|---|
| तुमने आम खाये। | *tumnē ām khāyē* | You ate mangoes. |
| उसने संतरे खाये। | *uṣnē santarē khāyē* | He ate oranges. |
| उसने मछली खायी। | *usnē machhlī khāyī* | He ate fish. |

In the sentences given above, the verb *khāyā* has changed throughout according to the number and gender of the objects--*rōṭī, rōṭiyāñ, kēlā, ām, santarē, machhlī etc.*

There are some irregular verbs which change differently for present perfect. They are *jānā* (to go), *dēnā* (to give) and *karnā* (to do).

*jānā* becomes *gayā* instead of *jayā.*

*maiñ gayā, āp gayē, vah gayā* and so on.

*dēnā* becomes *diyā* instead of *dēyā.*

*karnā* becomes *kiyā* and not *karyā.*

The last two are transitive verbs.

In Hindi *jāyī* is written as जायी or जाई, and *jāyē as* जाये or जाए। Both are correct.

**Present Perfect Continuous**

| | | |
|---|---|---|
| मैं जाता रहा हूं। | *maiñ jātā rahā hūñ* | I have been going. |
| मैं आपसे कहता रहा हूं। | *maiñ āpsē kahtā rahā hūñ* | I have been telling you. |
| वह आता रहा है। | *vah ātā rahā hai* | He has been coming. |

## Past Tense

### भूतकाल *(bhūt kāl)*

**Past Indefinite**

| | | |
|---|---|---|
| मैं जाता था। | *maiñ jātā thā* | I went. |

| | | |
|---|---|---|
| मैं जाती थी। | *maiñ jaātī thī* | I went. |
| हम जाते थे। | *ham jātē thē* | We went. |
| तुम जाते थे | *tum jātē thē* | You went. |
| आप जाते थे। | *āp jātē thē* | You went. |
| वह जाता था | *vah jātā thā* | He went. |
| वह जाती थी। | *vah jātī thī* | She went. |
| वे जाते थे। | *vē jātē thē* | They went. |

In the case of past indefinite, it is easier to remember the last auxiliary verbs as they follow a simpler pattern.

masculine singular — *thā* (was)
masculine plural — *thē* (were)
feminine singular — *thī* (was)
feminine plural — *thīñ*

The second person, of course, is always in plural.

Let us have more complete sentences :

| | |
|---|---|
| दिल्ली में मैं स्कूल जाता था।<br>*Dillī mēñ maiñ skūl jātā thā* | I went to school in Delhi. |
| गरमी में हम सैर करते थे।<br>*garmī mēñ ham sair kartē thē* | We went for walks in summer |
| वह सिर्फ इतवार को आती थी।<br>*vah sirf itvār kō ātī thī* | She came only on Sundays. |
| आप दिल्ली में क्या करते थे ?<br>*āp Dillī mēñ kyā kartē thē ?* | What did you do in Delhi ? |
| मैं दिल्ली में पढ़ता था।<br>*maiñ Dillī mēñ paḍhṭā thā* | I studied in Delhi. |
| आप क्या पढ़ते थे ?<br>*āp kyā paḍhtē thē ?* | What did you study ? |

| | |
|---|---|
| मैं हिन्दी पढ़ता था। <br> *māiñ Hindī paḍhtā thā* | I studied Hindī. |
| आप हिन्दी कहां पढ़ते थे ? <br> *āp Hindī kahāñ paḍhtē thē ?* | Where did you study Hindi ? |
| मैं विश्वविद्यालय में पढ़ता था। <br> *maiñ vishvavidyālaya mēñ paḍhtā thā* | I studied at the University. |
| पिछले साल मैं भी दिल्ली में था। <br> *pichhalē sāl maiñ bhī Dillī mēñ thā* | Last year I was also in Delhi. |
| क्या आप भी पढ़ते थे ? <br> *kyā āp bhī paḍhtē thē ?* | Did you study too ? |
| जी नहीं, मैं नौकरी करता था। <br> *jī nahiñ maiñ naukarī kartā thā* | No, I was in service. |
| आप कहां नौकरी करते थे ? <br> *āp kahāñ naukarī kartē thē ?* | Where were you working ? |
| मैं सरकारी अफसर था। <br> *maiñ sarkārī afsar thā* | I was a government officer. |

**New words**

| | | | |
|---|---|---|---|
| *kyā* | what | *paḍhnā* | to study, to read |
| *kahāñ* | where | *vishvavidyālaya* | university |
| *pichhalē sāl* | last year | *sarkārī* | governmental, of the government |
| *bhī* | also | | |
| *naukarī* | service | *afsar* | officer |

**Past Continuous**

| | | |
|---|---|---|
| मैं जा रहा था। | *maiñ jā rahā thā* | I was going. |
| मैं जा रही थी। | *maiñ jā rahī thī* | I was going. (f) |
| हम जा रहे थे। | *hum jā rahē thē* | We were going. |

| | | |
|---|---|---|
| तुम जा रहे थे। | *tum jā rahē thē* | You were going. |
| आप जा रहे थे। | *āp jā rahē thē* | You were going. |
| आप जा रहीं थीं। | *āp jā rahī thīñ* | You were going. (f) |
| वह जा रहा था। | *vah jā rahā thā* | He was going. |
| वह जा रही थी। | *vah jā rahī thī* | She was going. |
| वे जा रहे थे। | *vē jā rahē thē* | They were going. |
| वे जा रही थीं। | *vē jā rahī thīñ* | They were going. (f) |

Verbs in past continuous follow the same rule as in present continuous except that the auxiliary verb in the end is *thā, thī, thē* (was, were) instead of *hūñ, hai, haiñ* (am, is, are)

| | | |
|---|---|---|
| आप क्या कर रहे हैं ? | *āp kyā kar rahē haiñ ?* | What are you doing ? |
| मैं पत्र लिख रहा हूं। | *maiñ patra likh rahā hūñ ?* | I am writing a letter. |
| किसको पत्र लिख रहे हैं ? | *kiskō patra likh rahē haiñ ?* | To whom are you writing the letter ? |
| मैं अपनी मां को लिख रहा हूं। | *maiñ apnī māñ kō likh rahā hūñ* | I am writing to my mother. |
| आप पत्र हिन्दी में लिख रहे हैं ? | *āp patra Hindī mēñ likh rahē haiñ ?* | Are you writing the letter in Hindi ? |
| जी हां, आज-कल मैं हिन्दी सीख रहा हूं। | *jī hāñ, āj-kal maiñ Hindī sīkh rahā hūñ* | Yes, these days I am learning Hindi. |
| और मैं हिन्दी पढ़ा रहा हूं। | *aur maiñ Hindi paḍhā rahā hūñ* | And I am teaching Hindi. |

**New Words**

*patra* — letter

| | |
|---|---|
| *likhnā* | to write |
| *mā kō* | to mother |
| *apnī* | my |
| *Hindī mēñ* | in Hindi |
| *āj-kal* | these days |
| *sīkhnā* | to learn |
| *paḍhānā* | to teach |
| *aur* | and |

**Past Perfect**

| | | |
|---|---|---|
| मैं गया था। | *maiñ gayā thā* | I had gone. |
| मैं गयी थी। | *maiñ gayī thī* | I had gone. (f) |
| हम गये थे। | *ham gayē thē* | We had gone. |
| तुम गये थे। | *tum gayē thē* | You had gone. |
| आप गयी थीं। | *āp gayīñ thīñ* | You had gone (f) |
| वह गया था। | *vah gayā thā* | He had gone. |
| वह गयी थी। | *vah gayī thī* | She had gone. |
| वे गये थे। | *vē gayē thē* | They had gone. |
| वे गयी थीं। | *vē gayīñ thīñ* | They had gone. (f) |
| आप आज दफ्तर गये थे ? | *āp āj daftar gayē thē ?* | Did you go to office today ? |
| जी नहीं, मैं आज | *ji nahīñ, maiñ āj* | No, I did not go |
| दफ्तर नहीं गया था। | *daftar nahīñ gayā thā* | to office today. |
| मैं बाजार गया था। | *maiñ bāzār gayā thā* | I had gone to the market. |
| मैं आपके घर गया था। | *maiñ āpkē ghar gayā thā* | I went to your house. |

| | | |
|---|---|---|
| कल शाम आप कहां गये थे ? | *kal shām āp khān gayē thē ?* | Where did you go yesterday evening ? |
| कल बंबई से मेरा दोस्त आया था। | *kal Bambaī sē mērā dōst āyā thā* | Yesterday my friend had come from Bombay. |
| उसने कल मेरे साथ खाना खाया था। | *usnē kal mērē sāth khānā khāyā thā* | He had a meal with me yesterday. |
| मेरी पत्नी ने खाना पकाया था। | *mērī patnī nē khānā pakāyā thā* | My wife had cooked the meal. |

## Future Tense

(भविष्यत् काल *Bhavishyat kāl)*

| | | |
|---|---|---|
| मैं जाऊंगा। | *mai jāūñgā* | I shall go. (m) |
| मैं जाऊंगी। | *mai jāūñgī* | I shall go. (f) |
| हम जायेंगे। | *ham jāēñgē* | We shall go. |
| तुम जाओगे। | *tum jāōgē* | You shall go. |
| तुम जाओगी। | *tum jāōgī* | You shall go. (f) |
| आप जायेंगे। | *āp jāēñgē* | You shall go. |
| आप जायेंगी। | *āp jāēñgī* | You shall go. (f) |
| वह जायेगा। | *vah jāēga* | He will go. |
| वह जायेगी। | *vah jāēgī* | She will go. (f) |
| वे जायेंगे। | *vē jāēñgē* | They will go. |
| वे जायेंगी। | *vē jāēñgī* | They will go. (f) |

To form the future tense, add to the verb stem--

| | | |
|---|---|---|
| 1st person : | *ūñgā* | to masculine singular |
| | *ūñgī* | to feminine singular |
| | *ēñgē* | to masculine singular |
| | *ēñgī* | to feminine singular |

| | | |
|---|---|---|
| 2nd person : | *ōgē* | masculine singular and plural *(tum)* |
| | *ōgī* | feminine singular and plural *(tum)* |
| | *ēñgē* | masculine singular and plural *(āp)* |
| | *ēñgī* | feminine singular and plural *(āp)* |
| 3rd person : | *ēgā* | masculine singular |
| | *ēñgē* | masculine plural |
| | *ēgī* | feminine singular |
| | *ēñgī* | feminine plural |

| | |
|---|---|
| कल सवेरे आप घर पर होंगे ?<br>*kal savērē āp ghar par hōñgē ?* | Will you be at home tomorrow morning ? |
| आप कितने बजे आना चाहेंगे ?<br>*āp kitnē bajē ānā chāhēñgē ?* | At what time would you like to come ? |
| मैं आठ बजे आना चाहूंगा ।<br>*maiñ āṭh bajē ānā chāhūñgā* | I would like to come at eight o'clock. |
| आप नौ बजे आ सकेंगे ?<br>*āp nau bajē ā sakēñgē ?* | Will you be able to come at nine o'clock ? |
| जी हां, मैं नौ बजे आऊंगा ।<br>*jī hāñ, maiñ nau bajē āūñgā* | Yes, I shall come at nine o'clock. |
| मैं आपकी प्रतीक्षा करूंगा ।<br>*maiñ āpkī pratīkshā karūñgā* | I shall wait for you. |
| मैं ठीक नौ बजे पहुंचूंगा ।<br>*maiñ ṭhīk nau bajē pahuñchūñgā* | I shall reach exactly at nine o'clock. |

| | |
|---|---|
| धन्यवाद ! अब मैं जाऊंगा ।<br>*dhanyavād ! ab maiñ jāuñgā* | Thank you ! I shall go now. |
| आप चाय नहीं पिएंगे ?<br>*āp chāē nahiñ piēñgē ?* | Will you not take tea ? |
| जी नहीं, धन्यवाद । मैं सिर्फ ठंडा पानी पिऊंगा ।<br>*jī nahiñ, dhanyavād ! maiñ sirf ṭhanḍā pānī piūngā* | No thanks, I shall only drink cold water. |
| चाय में देर नहीं होगी । बिल्कुल तैयार है ।<br>*chāē mēñ dēr nahīñ hōgi, bilkul taiyār hai* | Tea will not take long. It is absolutely ready. |
| चाय के साथ कुछ खाएंगे ?<br>*Chāē kē sāth kuchh khāēñgē ?* | Will you have something to eat with tea ? |
| जी नहीं, धन्यवाद । अब मैं चलूंगा । देर हो जायेगी ।<br>*jī nahīñ, dhanyavād. ab maiñ chalūñgā. dēr hō jāēgī* | No thanks, Now I shall make a move. It will be late. |

**New Words**

| | |
|---|---|
| *savērē* | in the morning |
| *ghar par* | at home |
| *hoñgē* | will be |
| *kitne bajē* | at what o'clock |
| *chāhēñgē* | would like |
| *ā sakēñgē ?* | can you come ? |
| *pratīkshā karnā* | to wait |
| *pratīkshā (n)* | |

*contd. on page 74*

| Infinitive | | Present Indefinite | Present Continuous |
|---|---|---|---|
| जाना | I s* | (मैं) जाता हूं | जा रहा हूं |
| | | *(maiñ) jātā hūñ* | *jā rahā hūñ* |
| | p** | (हम) जाते हैं | जा रहे हैं |
| | | *(ham) jātē haiñ* | *jā rahē hain* |
| | II s | (तुम) जाते हो | जा रहे हो |
| | | *(tum) jātē hō* | *jā rahē hō* |
| | | (आप) जाते हैं | जा रहे हैं |
| | | *(āp) jātē haiñ* | *jā rahē haiñ* |
| | p | (आप लोग) जाते हैं | जा रहे हैं |
| | | *jātē haiñ* | *jā rahē haiñ* |
| | III s | (वह) जाता है | जा रहा है |
| | | *(vah) jātā hai* | *jā rahā hai* |
| | | (वे) जाते हैं | जा रहे हैं |
| | | *(vē) jātē haiñ* | *jā rahē haiñ* |
| आना | I s | (मैं) आता हूं | आ रहा हूं |
| | | *(maiñ) ātā hūñ* | *ā rahā hūñ* |
| | p | (हम) आते हैं | आ रहे हैं |
| | | *(ham) ātē haiñ* | *ā rahē haiñ* |
| | II s | (तुम) आते हो | आ रहे हो |
| | | *(tum) ātē hō* | *ā rahē hō* |
| | | (आप) आते हैं | आ रहे हैं |
| | | *(āp) ātē haiñ* | *ā rahē haiñ* |
| | III s | (वह) आता है | आ रहा है |
| | | *(vah) jātā hai* | *ā rahā hai* |
| | p | (वे) आते हैं | आ रहे हैं |
| | | *(ve) ātē haiñ* | *ā rahē haiñ* |

---

*s : singular, **p : Plural

# ERB CHART

| Present Perfect | Past Indefinite | Past Continuous | Past Perfect | Future |
|---|---|---|---|---|
| गया हूं | जाता था | जा रहा था | गया था | जाऊंगा |
| *gayā hūñ* | *jātā thā* | *jā rahā thā* | *gayā thā* | *jāūñgā* |
| गये हैं | जाते थे | जा रहे थे | गये थे | जाएंगे |
| *gayē haiñ* | *jātē thē* | *jā rahē thē* | *gayē thē* | *jāēñgē* |
| गये हो | जाते थे | जा रहे थे | गये थे | जाओगे |
| *gayē hō* | *jātē thē* | *jā rahē thē* | *gayē thē* | *jāōgē* |
| गये हैं | जाते थे | जा रहे थे | गये थे | जाएंगे |
| *gayē haiñ* | *jātē thē* | *jā rahē thē* | *gayē thē* | *jāēñgē* |
| गये हैं | जाते थे | जा रहे थे | गये थे | जाएंगे |
| *gayē haiñ* | *jātē thē* | *jā rahē thē* | *gayē thē* | *jāēñgē* |
| गया है | जाता था | जा रहा था | गया था | जाएगा |
| *gayā hai* | *jātā thā* | *jā rahā thā* | *gayā thā* | *jāegā* |
| गये हैं | जाते थे | जा रहे थे | गये थे | जाएंगे |
| *gayē haiñ* | *jātē thē* | *jā rahē thē* | *gayē thē* | *jāēñgē* |
| आया हूं | आता था | आ रहा था | आया था | आऊंगा |
| *āyā hūñ* | *ātā thā* | *ā rahā thā* | *āyā thā* | *āūñgā* |
| आये हैं | आते थे | आ रहे थे | आये थे | आएंगे |
| *āyē haiñ* | *ātē thē* | *ā rahē thē* | *āyē thē* | *āēñgē* |
| आये हो | आते थे | आ रहे थे | आये थे | आओगे |
| *āyē hō* | *ātē thē* | *ā rahē thē* | *āyē thē* | *āōgē* |
| आये हैं | आते थे | आ रहे थे | आये थे | आएंगे |
| *āyē haiñ* | *ātē thē* | *ā rahē thē* | *āyē thē* | *āēñgē* |
| आया है | आता था | आ रहा था | आया था | आएगा |
| *āyā hai* | *ātā thā* | *a rahā thā* | *āyā thā* | *āēga* |
| आये हैं | आते थे | आ रहे थे | आये थे | आएंगे |
| *āyē haiñ* | *ātē thē* | *ā rahē thē* | *āyē thē* | *āyeñge* |

*contd. from page 71*

| | |
|---|---|
| *piēñgē* | will drink |
| *dēr* | delay |
| *taiyār* | ready |
| *kuchh* | something |
| *chalūñgā* | shall move on, shall go |
| *hō jayēgī* | will happen |

**Request or Command**

This form of the verb in English is known as the imperative mood. The following examples will make it clear how this is formed. It is formed differently in the case of *tum* or *āp*. In the case of *tum* it may be a command or a wish. In the case of *āp* it may be a wish or a request as this form is the polite form. It would be more polite if *kirpayā* (please) is added in the beginning.

| | | |
|---|---|---|
| (तुम) दूध पिओ। | *(tum) dūdh piō* | Drink milk. |
| (तुम) रोटी खाओ। | *(tum) rōṭī khāō* | Eat bread. |
| गरम चाय लाओ। | *garam chāē lāo* | Bring hot tea. |
| (आप) दूध पीजिए। | *āp dūdh pijiyē* | Please drink milk. |
| (आप) रोटी खाइए। | *āp rōṭī khāiyē* | Please eat bread. |
| कृपया, अन्दर आइए। | *kripayā andar āiyē* | Please come in. |
| कृपया बैठिए। | *kripayā baiṭhiyē* | Please be seated. |

In the case of negative imperative, forbidding a person from doing something, *mat* is added before the verb.

| | | |
|---|---|---|
| फूल मत तोड़ो | *phūl mat tōṛō* | Don't pluck flowers. |
| गाड़ी तेज मत चलाओ। | *gāṛī tēz mat chalāō* | Don't drive the car fast. |
| कृपया ज़ोर से मत बोलिए। | *kripayā zōr sē mat bōliyē* | Please don't talk loudly. |

| | | |
|---|---|---|
| कृपया आप बाहर प्रतीक्षा कीजिए। | *kripayā āp bāhar pratīkshā kījiyē* | Please wait outside. |
| कृपया दरवाजा खोलिए। | *kripayā darvāzā khōliyē* | Please open the door. |
| कृपया कल शाम मेरे साथ खाना खाइए। | *kripayā kal shām mērē sāth khānā khāiyē* | Please have dinner with me tomorrow evening. |
| आप मेरे साथ चलिए। | *āp mērē sāth chaliyē* | Please come with me. |
| बाहर मत जाइए। | *bāhar mat jāiyē* | Don't go out. |
| बच्चों, बारिश में मत खेलो। | *bachchōñ, bārish mēñ mat khēlō* | Children, don't play in the rain. |

Given below are some common verbs and their imperative form. Readers are advised to use them in sentences as an exercise.

| | | | |
|---|---|---|---|
| आना | *ānā* | आओ, आइए | *āō, aiyē* |
| जाना | *jānā* | जाओ, जाइए | *jāō, jāiyē* |
| खाना | *khānā* | खाओ, खाइए | *khāō, khāiyē* |
| देखना | *dēkhnā* | देखो, देखिए | *dēkhō, dēkhiyē* |
| लिखना | *likhanā* | लिखो, लिखिए | *likhō, likhiyē* |
| पढ़ना | *paḍhnā* | पढ़ो, पढ़िए | *paḍhō, paḍhiyē* |
| गाना | *gānā* | गाओ, गाइए | *gāō, gāiyē* |
| करना | *karnā* | करो, कीजिए | *karō, kījiyē* |
| पीना | *pīnā* | पीओ, पीजिए | *pīō, pījiyē* |
| लेना | *lēnā* | लो, लीजिए | *lō, lījiyē* |
| बोलना | *bōlnā* | बोलो, बोलिए | *bōlō, boliyē* |
| सुनना | *sunanā* | सुनो, सुनिए | *sunō, suniyē* |

*pījiyē, kījiyē, lījiyē* and *khaiyē* etc. are irregular as seen from the examples above.

Sometimes indefinite is used as imperative in second person *(tum)*.

| | | |
|---|---|---|
| बाहर मत जाना। | *bāhar mat jānā* | Don't go out. |
| एक गिलास पानी लाना। | *ēk gilās pānī lānā* | Bring a glass of water. |
| खाना गरम करना। | *khānā garam karnā* | Warm up the food. |
| फल काटना। | *phal kāṭnā* | Cut the fruits. |

**Subjunctive Mood**

When a verb is in a subjunctive mood, usually the sentence has two clauses; the verb in one of the clauses is in the subjunctive mood, that is, it lays down a condition, a wish or a purpose.

मैंने उसको पैसे दिए जिससे वह खाना खा सके।
*māiñē uskō paisē diyē jissē vah khānā khā sakē*
I gave him money so that he may eat food.

मैंने तुम्हारा वेतन बढ़ाया जिससे तुम ज्यादा अच्छा काम करो।
*māiñē tumhārā vētan baḍhāyā jissē tum zyādā achchhā kām karō*
I raised your pay so that you may work better.

मैंने आग जलायी जिससे कमरा गरम हो जाये।
*māiñē āg jalāyī jissē kamrā garam hō jāē*
I lit the fire so that the room becomes warm.

**New Words**

| | |
|---|---|
| *paisē* | paise, money |
| *jissē* | so that |
| *khā sakē* | can eat |
| *vētan* | pay, wage |

| | |
|---|---|
| *baḍhāyā* | raised, increased |
| *zyādā achchhā* | better |
| *karō* | do |
| *āg* | fire |
| *jalāyī* | lit |
| *hō jāē* | becomes |

Another form of conditional verb :

अगर आप आएं तो मेरी किताब ले आएं।

*agar āp āyēñ tō mērī kitāb lē ayēñ*

If you come, please bring my book.

अगर वह आए तो उसे मेरे पास भेज दें।

*agar vah āyē tō usē mērē pȧs bhēj dēñ*

If he comes, please send him to me.

अगर वह भूखा हो तो उसे रोटी दे दें।

*agar vah bhūkhā hō tō usē rōṭi dē dēñ*

If he is hungry, give him bread.

अगर मेरे गुरु जी आएं तो कमरे में बिठा देना।

*agar mērē gurujī āyēñ tō kamarē mēñ biṭhā dēnā*

If my teacher comes, make him sit in the room.

These sentences have doubt clauses too. The first clause expresses a doubt, if this happens, and the second clause gives an order or makes a request.

**Interrogative Words**

| | | |
|---|---|---|
| कौन | *kaun* | who |
| क्या | *kyā* | what |
| क्यों | *kyōñ* | why |
| कब | *kab* | when |
| कब तक | *kab tak* | until when, by what time |

| | | |
|---|---|---|
| कहां | *kahāñ* | where |
| कैसे | *kaisē* | how |
| कौन-सा | *kaun-sā* | which, which one |
| किसको | *kiskō* | whom |
| किसका | *kiskā* | whose |
| कितना | *kitanā* | how much |
| कितने | *kitanē* | how many |

It is interesting that all the interrogative words begin with *kā*. Now let us use them in sentences.

यह आदमी कौन है ? — Who is this man ?
*yah ādmī kaun hai ?*

उसका नाम क्या है ? — What is his name ?
*uskā nām kyā hai ?*

वह क्यों आया है ? — Why has he come ?
*vah kyōñ āyā hai ?*

वह कब जाएगा ? — When will he go ?
*vah kab jāyēgā ?*

वह कब तक रहेगा ? — How long will he stay ?
*vah kab tak rahēgā ?*

आप कहां जा रहे ? — Where are you going ?
*āp kahāñ jā rahē haiñ ?*

आप कैसे हैं ? — How are you ?
*āp kaisē haiñ ?*

आपकी कलम कौन-सी है ? — Which one is your pen ?
*āpkī kalam kaun-sī hai*

आप यह किताब किसको देंगे ? — To whom wilk you give this book ?
*āp yah kitāb kiskō dēñgē ?*

| | |
|---|---|
| यह किसका मकान है ?<br>*yah kiskā makān hai ?* | Whose house is this ? |
| आपके पास कितने रुपये हैं ?<br>*āpkē pās kitanē rupayē haiñ ?* | How many rupees do you have ? |
| आपको कितना आटा चाहिए ?<br>*āpkō kitnā āṭā chāhiē ?* | How much flour do you want ? |
| मुझको पानी चाहिए ।<br>*mujhkō pānī chāhiē* | I want water. |
| मुझको एक किलो आलू चाहिए ।<br>*mujhkō ēk kilō ālū chāhiē* | I want a kilo of potatoes. |
| आपको क्या चाहिए ?<br>*āpkō kyā chāhiē ?* | What do you want ? |
| बच्चे को खिलौना चाहिए ।<br>*bachchē kō khilaunā chāhiē* | The child wants a toy. |
| बच्चा भूखा है, उसको दूध चाहिए ।<br>*bachcha bhūkhā hai, uskō dūdh chāhiē* | The child is hungry, he wants milk. |
| उसको यह कपड़ा दो मीटर चाहिए ।<br>*uskō yah kapḍa dō mītar chāhiē* | He wants two metres of this cloth. |

*Chāhiē* is a word you are likely to use very often. It is important to note the construction of a sentence with *chāhiē* which means needed or wanted. Literally translated into English it would mean wanted or needed by me e.g. one kilo of potatoes is needed by me.

**Can, Could**

सकना *sakanā* (to be able to)

**Present Tense**

| | |
|---|---|
| आप हिन्दी बोल सकते हैं ?<br>*āp Hindī bōl sakatē haiñ ?* | Can you speak Hindi ? |
| जी हाँ, मैं कुछ-कुछ बोल सकता हूं ।<br>*jī hāñ, maiñ kuchh-kuchh bōl sakatā hūñ* | Yes, I can speak a little. |
| लेकिन, मैं अच्छी तरह समझ सकता हूं ।<br>*lēkin, maiñ ahhchhī tarah samajh sakatā hūñ* | But, I can understand well. |
| आप पढ़ भी सकते हैं ?<br>*āp paḍh bhī sakatē haiñ ?* | Can you also read ? |
| जी नहीं, मैं पढ़ या लिख नहीं सकता ।<br>*jī nahīñ, maiñ paḍh yā likh nahīñ sakatā* | No, I cannot read or write. |

**Future Tense**

| | |
|---|---|
| आप आज शाम मेरे घर आ सकेंगे ?<br>*āp āj shām mērē ghar ā sakēñgē ?* | Will you be able to come to my house this evening ? |
| मुझको अफसोस है, मैं नहीं आ सकूँगा ।<br>*mujhkō afsōs hai, maiñ nahīñ ā sakūngā* | I am sorry, I shall not be able to come. |
| आप अभी पाँच मिनट में तैयार हो सकेंगे ?<br>*āp abhī pañch minat mēñ taiyār hō sakēñgē ?* | Can you get ready now within five minutes ? |

आप गा सकते हैं ?
*āp gā saktē haiñ ?*

Can you sing ?

मैं सिर्फ बंगाली गीत गा सकता हूं ।
*maiñ sirf Bangālī gīt gā saktā hūñ*

I can sing only Bengali songs.

**Past Tense**

मैं जा सकता था, लेकिन गया नहीं ।
*maiñ jā saktā thā, lēkin gayā nahīñ*

I could have gone, but I did not go.

मैं नहीं जा सका ।
*maiñ nahīñ jā sakā*

I could not go.

मैं नहीं देख सका ।
*maiñ nahīñ dēkh sakā*

I was not able to see.

माफ कीजिए, मैं कल नहीं आ सका ।
*māf kījiyē, maiñ kal nahīñ ā sakā*

Forgive me, I could not come yesterday.

Another interesting variation in Hindi is in the verb, to like--*pasand karnā.* It is formed by two words. Usually it is used in a passive manner of speech. For example, I like mangoes (would be) *mujhkō ām pasand haiñ.*

मुझको नाचना पसंद है ।
*mujhkō nāchanā pasand hai*

I like to dance.

मुझको दिल्ली पसंद है ।
*mujhkō Dillī pasand hai*

I like Delhi.

आपको कौन-सा फल सबसे ज्यादा पसंद है ?
*āpkō kaun-sā phal sabsē zyādā pasand hia ?*

Which fruit do you like the most ?

मुझको सेब सबसे ज्यादा पसंद है।
*mujhkō sēb sub sē zyādā pasand hai*
I like apples the most. (more than all others).

आपको मसालेदार खाना पसंद है ?
*āpkō masālēdār khānā pasand hai ?*
Do you like spicy food?

मुझको ज्यादा मसाला पसंद नहीं है।
*mujhkō zyādā masālā pasand nahiñ hai*
I do not like too much spice.

**New Words**

| | |
|---|---|
| *bōl (nā)* | to speak |
| *kuchh-kuchh* | a little, somewhat |
| *samajh (nā)* | understand |
| *achchhī tarah* | well, properly |
| *paḍh (nā)* | read |
| *likh (nā)* | write |
| *afsōs* | regret |
| *taiyār* | ready |
| *hōnā* | to be |
| *gā* | sing |
| *gīt* | song |
| *lēkin* | but |
| *māf kījiyē* | excuse me, forgive me |
| *nāchanā* | to dance |
| *sēb* | apple |
| *masālēdār* | spicy |

## Transitive and Intransitive Verbs

| Intransitive | | | Transitive | | |
|---|---|---|---|---|---|
| सोना | *sōnā* | to sleep | सुलाना | *sulānā* | to put to sleep |
| हंसना | *hañṣnā* | to laugh | हंसाना | *hañsānā* | to make others laugh |
| रोना | *rōnā* | to weep | रुलाना | *rulānā* | to make someone weep |
| खेलना | *khēlnā* | to play | खिलाना | *khelānā* | to make someone play |
| उठना | *uṭhnā* | to get up | उठाना | *uṭhānā* | to make someone get up, or to wake up someone, or to lift |
| जीना | *jīnā* | to live | जिलाना | *jīlānā* | to give life to someone |
| कटना | *kaṭnā* | to cut | काटना | *kāṭanā* | to cut |
| नाचना | *nāchanā* | to dance | नचाना | *nachānā* | to make someone dance |
| मरना | *marnā* | to die | मारना | *mārnā* | to kill, to beat |
| पिटना | *piṭnā* | to be beaten up | पीटना | *pītnā* | to beat |
| डरना | *ḍarnā* | to fear | डराना | *ḍarānā* | to frighten |
| चिढ़ना | *chiḍhnā* | to be teased | चिढ़ाना | *chiḍhānā* | to tease |

**Examples :**

| | | |
|---|---|---|
| मैं डर गया। | *maiñ ḍar gayā* | I was frightened. |
| मैंने उसको डरा दिया। | *mainē uskō ḍarā diyā* | I frightened him. |
| मैं हंसा। | *maiñ hañsā* | I laughed. |
| मैंने उसको हंसाया। | *mainē uskō hañsāyā* | I made him laugh. |
| मैं खेल रहा हूं। | *maiñ khēl rahā hūñ* | I am playing. |
| मैं बच्चों को खिला रहा हूं। | *maiñ bachchōñ kō khilā rahā hūñ* | I am making the children play. |
| मैं सो रहा था। | *maiñ sō rahā thā* | I was sleeping. |
| मैं बच्चे को सुला रहा था। | *maiñ bachchē kō sulā rahā thā* | I was putting the child to sleep. |
| तुम क्यों रो रहे हो ? | *tum kyōñ rō rahē hō ?* | Why are you crying ? |
| तुम उसे क्यों रुला रहे हो ? | *tum usē kyōñ rulā rahē hō ?* | Why are you making him cry ? |
| वह मुझको चिढ़ाता है। | *vah mujhkō chiḍhātā hai* | He teases me. |

| Transitive | | | Causative | | |
|---|---|---|---|---|---|
| करना | *karnā* | to do | करवाना | *karvānā* | to make someone do |
| पीना | *pīnā* | to drink | पिलवाना | *pilvānā* | to make someome drink |
| खाना | *khānā* | to eat | खिलाना | *khilānā* | to feed |
| सुनना | *sunanā* | to hear | सुनाना | *sunānā* | to narrate |
| देखना | *dēkhanā* | to see | दिखाना | *dikhānā* | to show |
| सीना | *sīnā* | to sew | सिलाना | *silānā* | to get someone to sew |
| पकाना | *pakānā* | to cook | पकवाना | *pakavānā* | to get cooked |
| मारना | *māranā* | to beat | मरवाना | *maravānā* | to get someone to beat |

**Examples :**

| | | |
|---|---|---|
| मैंने काम किया। | *mainē kām kiyā* | I did the work. |
| मैंने काम करवाया। | *mainē kām karavāyā* | I got the work done. |
| मैंने रोटी खायी। | *mainē rōṭī khāyī* | I ate bread. |

| | | |
|---|---|---|
| मैंने उसको रोटी खिलवायी। | *mainē usakō rōṭī khilavāyī* | I fed him bread. |
| मैंने एक कहानी सुनी | *mainē ēka kahānī sunī* | I heard a story. |
| मैंने उसको कहानी सुनवायी। | *mainē usakō kahānī sunavāyī* | I narrated him a story. |
| मैंने तस्वीर देखी। | *mainē tasvīra dēkhī* | I saw the picture. |
| मैंने तस्वीर दिखायी। | *mainē tasvīra dikhāyī* | I showed the picture. |
| मैंने उसको मारा | *mainē usakō mārā* | I beat him. |
| मैंने उसको मरवाया। | *mainē usakō maravāyā* | I got him beaten up. |

CHAPTER EIGHT

# ADVERBS

## क्रिया विशेषण *(Kriya Vishēṣhaṇ)*

| | |
|---|---|
| चाय बहुत गरम है। <br> *Chāē bahut garam hai* | Tea is very hot. |
| वह तेज़ चलता है। <br> *vah tēz chaltā hai* | He walks fast. |
| मुझको बिल्कुल नहीं मालूम। <br> *mujhkō bilkul nahīn mālūm* | It is not known to me at all. |
| मैं वहां जा रहा हूं। <br> *maiñ vahāñ jā rahā hūñ* | I am going there. |
| वह काफी दूर चला गया। <br> *vah kāfi dūr chalā gayā* | He has gone quite far away. |
| वह फ़ौरन आ गया। <br> *vah fauran ā gayā* | He came immediately. |

An adverb precedes the verb or adjective it qualifies as seen in the examples given above.

Sometimes an adverb is repeated to emphasise and also for effectiveness of speech.

| | |
|---|---|
| जल्दी-जल्दी काम करो। <br> *jaldī-jaldī kām karō* | Work fast. |
| धीरे-धीरे खाओ। <br> *dhīrē-dhīrē khāō* | Eat slowly. |

| | |
|---|---|
| धीरे-धीरे बोलिए ।<br>*dhīrē-dhirē bōliyē* | Speak slowly. |
| आप कहाँ-कहाँ जायेंगे ?<br>*āp kahāñ-kahāñ jāeñgē ?* | Which are the places you will go to ? |
| वह कब-कब आता है ?<br>*vah kab-kab ātā hai ?* | When does he come ? (What are the days or times when he comes ?) |

Another thing to remember is that where words like above *(ūpar)* or below *(nīchē)* are used they are preceded by a preposition.

**Examples :**

| | |
|---|---|
| मेज़ के ऊपर<br>*mēz kē ūpar* | on the table |
| मेज़ के नीचे<br>*mēz kē nīchē* | under the table |
| घर के चारों ओर<br>*ghar kē chārōñ ōr* | around the house or all the four sides of the house |
| नदी के पार<br>*nadī kē pār* | beyond the river |
| नदी के उस पार<br>*nadī kē us pār* | on the other side of the river |
| नदी के किनारे<br>*nadī kē kinārē* | on the riverside |
| ज़मीन के नीचे<br>*zamīn kē nīchē* | under the ground |

| | |
|---|---|
| घर के पास<br>*ghar kē pās* | near the house |
| घर से दूर<br>*ghar sē dūr* | far from the house |
| उसके बारे में<br>*uskē bārē mēñ* | about him. |
| घर के सामने<br>*ghar kē sāmnē* | in front of the house |
| घर के पीछे<br>*ghar kē pīchhē* | behind the house |
| दो घरों के बीच में<br>*dō gharōñ kē bīch mēñ* | between two houses |
| शहर के बीचोबीच<br>*shahar kē bīchōbīch* | right in the centre of the town |
| बाग के ठीक बीच में<br>*bāg kē ṭhīk bīch mēñ* | right in the centre of the garden |
| वे साथ-साथ गए ।<br>*vē sāth-sāth gayē* | They went togther |
| वे अलग-अलग गए ।<br>*vē alag-alag gayē* | They went separately |
| वे एक साथ गए ।<br>*vē ek sāth gayē* | They went together |
| घर के आस-पास दुकानें हैं ।<br>*ghar kē ās-pās dukānēñ haiñ* | There are shops near about the house |

**Reading Exercise I**

आपके घर के सामने कौन रहता है ?

*āpkē ghar kē sāmnē kaun rahatā hai ?*

Who lives in front of your house.

मेरे बाग के बीचोबीच फव्वारा है।

*mērē bāg kē bīchō bīch phavvārā hai*

There is a fountain right in the centre of my garden.

मेरा कमरा अलग है।

*mērā kamarā alag hai*

My room is separate.

मेरे घर के पास बाज़ार है।

*mērē ghar kē pās bāzār hai*

There is a market near my house.

मेरे घर के आस-पास कई दुकानें हैं।

*mērē ghar kē ās-pās kaī dukanēñ haiñ*

There are several shops near about my house.

आपके घर के ऊपर कौन रहता है ?

*āpkē ghar kē ūpar kaun rahatā hai ?*

Who lives above your house ?

आपकी मेज़ के नीचे बिल्ली है।

*āpkī mēz ke nīchē billī hai.*

There is a cat under your table.

घरों के बीच में बाग है।

*gharōñ kē bīch mēñ bāg hai*

There is a garden in between the houses.

राम और सीता साथ-साथ स्कूल गए।
*Rām aur Sītā sāth-sāth skūl gayē*
Ram and Sita went to school together.

इन चीज़ों को एक साथ मत रखो।
*in chīzōñ kō ēk sāth mat rakhō*
Don't keep these things together.

नदी के उस पार जंगल है।
*nadī kē us pār jañgal hai*
There is a forest on the other side of the river.

मेरा घर नदी के किनारे है।
*mēra ghar nadī kē kinare hai*
My house is by the side of the river.

मेरा दफ्तर घर से दूर है।
*mērā daftar ghar sē dūr hai*
My office is far away from the house.

मेरा घर स्कूल के पास है।
*mērā ghar skūl kē pās hai*
My house is near the school.

मेरा घर स्कूल से ज़्यादा दूर नहीं है।
*mērā ghar skūl sē zyādā dūr nahīñ hai*
My house is not very far from the school.

मेरे घर के चारों ओर आम के पेड़ हैं।
*mērē ghar kē chārō ōr āmı kē pēḍ haiñ*
There are mango trees all around my house.

**Telling the Time**

कितने बजे हैं ? What time is it ?
*kitanē bajē haiñ ?*

| | |
|---|---|
| क्या वक्त है ?<br>*kyā vakt hai ?* | What is the time ? |
| क्या समय है ?<br>*kyā samaya hai ?* | What is the time ? |
| एक बजा है ।<br>*ek bajā hai* | It is one O' clock. |
| डेढ़ बजे हैं ।<br>*ḍēḍh bajē haiñ* | It is half past one. |
| दो बजे हैं ।<br>*dō bajē haiñ* | It is two O'clock. |
| ढाई बजे हैं ।<br>*ḍhaī bajē haiñ* | It is half past two. |
| तीन बजे हैं ।<br>*tīn bajē haiñ* | It is three O'clock. |
| सवा तीन बजे हैं ।<br>*savā tīn bajē haiñ* | It is quarter past three. |
| साढ़े चार बजे हैं ।<br>*sāḍhē chār bajē haiñ* | It is half past four. |
| पौने पांच बजे हैं ।<br>*paunē pāñch bajē haiñ* | It is a quarter to five. |

Note that a quarter is *savā.* Half or half past in respect of time, weight or measurement is *sāḍhē, paunē* is three-fourth or three quarters. Three and a half metres will be *sāḍhē tīn mīṭar,* three and three-fourth metre will be *paunē chār mīṭar,* four and a quarter metre will be *savā chār mīṭar* and so on.

Please also note one and a half is not *sāḍhē ēk* but *dēḍh;* similarly, two and a half is not *saḍhē dō* but *ḍhāī.*

तीन बजने में पांच मिनट हैं।
*tīn bajnē mēñ pāñch minat haiñ*
It is five minutes to three.

तीन बजकर दस मिनट।
*tīn baj kar das minat naiñ*
It is ten minutes past three.

मेरा दफ्तर दस बजे से पांच बजे तक होता है।
*mērā daftar das bajē sē pāñch bajē tak hōtā hai*
My office is from ten o'clock to five o'clock.

मेरी घड़ी पांच मिनट तेज़ है।
*mērī ghaḍī pāñch minaṭ tez hai*
My watch is fast by five minutes.

मेरी घड़ी आगे है।
*mērī ghaḍī āgē hai*
My watch is fast.

मेरी घड़ी पांच मिनट पीछे है।
*mērī ghaḍī pāñch minaṭ pīchhē hai*
My watch is slow by five minutes.

मेरी घड़ी बंद है।
*mērī ghaḍī band hai*
My watch is closed. (literal meaning)

मेरी घड़ी रुक गयी है।
*mērī ghaḍī ruk gayī hai*
My watch has stopped.

आप की घड़ी ठीक है ?
*āpkī ghaḍī thīk hai ?*
Is your watch correct ?

मेरी घड़ी खराब है।

*mērī ghaḍī kharāb hai*

My watch is bad i. e. it is not working.

मेरी घड़ी चल नहीं रही है।

*mērī ghaṛī chal nahīñ rahī hai*

My watch is not working.

**New words**

| | |
|---|---|
| *kitanē* | how many |
| *vakt, samay (m)* | time |
| *savā* | quarter |
| *dēḍh* | two-and-a-half |
| *paunē* | three quarters |

(*paunē pānch* would mean four and three quarters.)

| | |
|---|---|
| *ghaḍī* (f) | watch |
| *pīchhē* | behind |
| *āgē* | ahead |
| *rukanā* | to stop |
| *chalanā* | to move |
| *ghaḍīsāz* | watchmaker |

**Some common idioms**

लगा *lagā*

वह बोलने लगा — He began to speak.

*vah bōlnē lagā*

Although it would be quite grammatical and correct to say *usnē bōlnā shurū kiyā* (he started speaking) but it is more idiomatic to say *vah bōlnē lagā.* It would not be possible to translate this idiom into English as there is nothing equivalent. It would be helpful to understand in what different meanings the word *lagā* can be used, and then to try and use them. When learning a language, one should always try and use the idioms in that language though it may be difficult to translate them into one's own mother tongue.

मेरा बच्चा अब चलने लगा है।
*mērā bachchā ab chalnē lagā hai.*
My child has now started walking.

जैसे ही मैं घर से निकला, बारिश होने लगी।
As soon as I came out of the house, it started raining.
*jaisē hī maiñ ghar sē nikala, bārish hōnē lagī*

आपका बच्चा बोलने लगा ?
*āpkā bachchā bōlnē lagā ?*
Has your child started speaking ?

मेरा बच्चा चलने लगा है।
*mērā bachchā chalnē lagā hai.*
My child has started walking.

बारिश होने लगी।
*bārish hōnē lagī*
It has started raining.

When '*laganā*' is used as the principal verb, it means it "appears' or it 'feels'.

**Examples :**

मुझको ठण्ड लगती है। I feel cold
*mujhkō ṭhanḍ lagatī hai*

| | |
|---|---|
| उसको भूख लग रही है।<br>*uskō bhūkh lag rahī hai* | He is feeling hungry. |
| बच्चे को प्यास लग रही है।<br>*bachchē kō pyās lag rahī hai* | The child is feeling thirsty. |
| मुझको नींद लग रही है।<br>*mujhkō nīñd lag rahī hai* | I am feeling sleepy. |
| मुझको लगता है कि वह नहीं आएगा।<br>*mujhkō lagatā hai ki vah nahīñ ayēgā* | I feel he won't come. |
| मुझको लगता है मेरा पत्र आज जरूर आयेगा।<br>*mujhkō lagatā hai mērā patra āj zarūr ayēgā* | I feel my letter will definitely come today. |
| मुझको बरसात अच्छी नहीं लगता।<br>*mujhkō barsāt achchhī nahīñ lagatī* | I do not like the rainy season. |
| आपको चाय ज़्यादा अच्छी लगती है या कॉफी ?<br>*āpkō chāē zyādā achchhī lagatī hai yā kafī ?* | Which do you like better--tea or coffee ? |
| मुझको बाग में काम करना अच्छा लगता है।<br>*mujhkō bāg mēñ kām karnā achchhā lagatā hai* | I like to work in the garden. |
| गीता सुन्दर लग रही है।<br>*Gītā sundar lag rahī hai* | Gita is looking pretty. |
| यह आदमी गरीब लगता है।<br>*yah ādmī garīb lagatā hai* | This man appears to be poor. |

| | |
|---|---|
| यह आदमी चालाक लगता है। *yah ādmī chālāk lagatā hai* | This man appears to be cunning. |
| लगता है वह सो गया। *lagatā hai vah sō gayā* | It appears that he has gone to sleep. |
| लगता है वह चला गया। *lagatā hai vah chalā gayā* | It appears that he has left. |
| लगता है वह खा चुका। *lagatā hai vah khā chukā* | It appears that he has already eaten. |
| लगता है उसने पत्र नहीं पढ़ा। *lagatā hai usnē patra nahīn paḍhā* | It appears he has not read the letter. |

Note : It should be noted that when a sentence is negative, i. e., it has the word *nahīñ*, the auxiliary verb is often dropped.

Two verbs are often used together. For example :

| | |
|---|---|
| मैं जाना चाहता हूं। *maiñ jānā chāhtā hūñ* | I wish to go. |
| वह क्या खाना चाहता है ? *vah kyā khānā chāhtā hai ?* | What does he wish to eat ? |

When *lagā* is used with another verb, like *mērā bachchā chalanē lagā,* the first verb is invariably in the form *chanē, khānē, sōnē, pīnē* etc., irrespective of the gender, person or number of the subject, noun or pronoun. It is the verb *lagā* which changes according to the subject.

**Examples :**

*Present*

*maiñ*...................... *lagtā hūñ* (m)

*maiñ*...................... *lagtī hūñ* (f)

*ham*...................... *lagtē haiñ* (m)

*vah*...................... *lagtā hai* and so on.

*Future*

*maiñ*...................... *lagūñgā, lagūñgī* (m, f.)

*ham*...................... *lagēñgē*

*vah*...................... *lagēga, lagēgī*

*ve*...................... *lagēñgē*

*tum*...................... *lagōgē*

*āp*...................... *lagēñgē, lagēñgī*

**Examples :**

मैं कल से दफ्तर जाने लगूँगा।
*main kal sē daftar jānē lagūñgā*
I shall start going to the office from tomorrow.

वह कल से काम करने लगेगा।
*vah kal sē kām karnē lagēgā*
He will start working from tomorrow.

आप कब से स्कूल जाने लगेंगी ?
*āp kab sē skūl jānē lagēñgī ?*
When will you start going to the school ?

अन्दर बैठिए, बाहर ठंड लगेगी।
Sit inside, it will be cold outside.
*andar baiṭhiyē, bāhar ṭhanḍ lagēgī*

近期内鞏固比發展您的事業更有利。

रोटी खाइए नहीं तो भूख लगेगी।
*rōṭī khāiyē, nahīñ tō bhūkh lagēgī*
Eat bread, otherwise you will feel hungry.

*Past Tense*

आपको ठंड लगी ? — Did you feel cold ?
*āpkō ṭhanḍ lagī ?*

आपको यह शहर अच्छा लगा ? — Did you like this city ?
*āpkō yah shahar achchhā lagā ?*

वे कब से काम पर जाने लगे ? — When did they start going to work ?
*ve kab sē kām par jānē lagē ?*

*chāhnā* means to wish or to want. If it is used by itself, e : राम सीता को चाहता है। *Rām Sītā kō chāhtā hai.* It means m is fond of Sita. Or, *maiñ apnī billī kō bahut chāhtī hūñ,* ( I e my cat very much). But when it is combined with ther verb as given above, it means to want or to wish. The verb is always used in the infinitve form *jānā, ānā, gānā,* so on. It is the second verb *chāhtā* which will keep ging its form to agree with the number, gender or the on of the subject.

**ples :**

म चाय पीना चाहता हूं। — I want to drink tea.
*maiñ chāē pīnā chāhtā hūñ*

मैं आपका गाना सुनना चाहती हूं। — I want to hear you sing.
*maiñ āpkā gānā sunanā chāhtī hūñ*

वह मेरे घर आना चाहता है। — He wants to come to my house.
*vah mērē ghar ānā chāhta hai*

बच्चे बाहर खेलना चाहते हैं। *bachchē bāhar khēlanā chāthtē haiñ* — Childern want to play outside.

## चुकना *Chukanā*

*Chukanā* means to finish. It is added to a verb to mean finishing a job or the end of something.

मैं खा चुका। *maiñ khā chukā* — I have finished my meal.

मैं चाय पी चुका। *maiñ chāē pī chukā* — I have already had tea.

मैं यह फिल्म देख चुका। *maiñ yah film dēkh chukā* — I have already seen this film.

वह काम कर चुका ? *vah kām kar chukā ?* — Has he finished the job ?

आप खाना पका चुके ? *āp khānā pakā chukē ?* — Have you finished cooking ?

The word *chukā* may also be used with an adjective, but in that case it is usually combined with *hō*.

**Examples :**

काम खत्म हो चुका ? *[illegible]khatm hō chukā ?* — Has the work been completed ?

[illegible] चुका। — The food has become cold.

जब मैं खाने बैठी, खाना ठंडा हो चुका था।
When I sat down to eat, the food had already got cold.
*jab maiñ khānē baiṭhī, khānā ṭhanḍā hō chukā thā*

जब मैं चली तो बारिश खतम हो चुकी थी।
*jab maiñ chalī tō bārish khatam hō chukī thī*
When I started, the rain had already stopped.

जब मैं आया तो वह जा चुके थे।
When I came he had already left.
*jab maiñ āyā tō vah jā chukē thē*

*'Chukā'* adds the sense of finality to the meaning.

*Future Tense*

वह जा चुके होंगे।
*vah jā chukē hōñgē*
He will have gone *or* he must have gone.

वह खा चुकी होंगी।
*vah khā chukī hōñgī*
She will have finished her meal.

काम खत्म हो गया होगा।
*kām khatm hō gayā hōgā*
The work will have been finished.

वह किताब पढ़ चुका होगा।
*vah kitāb paḍh chukā hōgā*
He will have finised reading the book.

कल इस समय तक मैं जा चुकी होऊंगी।
*kal is samaya tak maiñ jā chukī hōuñgī*
Tomorrow by this time I will have gone.

मैंने सोचा आप खाना खा चुके होंगे।
*maiñē sōchā āp khāna khā chukē hōñgē*
I thought you must have finished eating.
मैंने सोचा आप यह किताब पढ़ चुके होंगे।
I thought you must have readthis book.
*maiñē sōchā āp kitāb paḍh chukē hōñgē*

The use of ही *hī* and तो *tō*

*Hī* is often used to emphasise a word in its exclusiveness.

**Examples :**
सिर्फ आप ही अन्दर आ सकते हैं।
*sirf āp hī andar ā sakatē haiñ*
Only you can come in.
मैं सिर्फ रोटी ही खाऊँगा।
*maiñ sirf roṭī hī khāūñgā*
I shall only eat bread.
आप आज काम ही करते रहेंगे ? खाना नहीं खाएँगे ?
*āp āj kām hī karatē rahēñgē, khānā nahīñ khayēñge ?*
Will you only keep working today ? Will you not eat ?

*tō* is sometimes used to mean then, or after, and sometimes it is used only for emphasis. It has no equivalent in English.

**Example :** (When it means then or if)
आप जाएंगे तो मैं भी जाऊंगा।
*āp jāyēñgē tō maiñ bhī jāūñgā*
If you go, I shall go too.

वह आएगा तो उसको किताब दे देना।
When he comes (then) give him the book.
*vah āyegā tō uskō kitāb dē dēnā*

अगर वह मांगे तो उसको दूध दे देना।
If he asks, (then) give him milk.
*agar vah māñgē tō uskō dūdh dē dēnā*

आप खा चुकें तो यहां आइएगा।
*āp khā chukēñ tō yahāñ āiyēgā*
When you finish eating, (then) please come here/(come when you have finished eating).

वह बुलाए तो जाना।
*vah bulāē tō jānā*
If he calls you (then) go. (Go if he calls you)

वह पैसे दे तो मत लेना।
*vah paisē dē tō mat lēnā*
If he gives money, don't take it.

In the last two sentences given above, the infinitive form of the verb, *jānā* and *lēnā* is used as imperative. It has already been mentioned earlier in the chapter on verbs that infinitive can be used as imperative with *tum*.

*tō* is used here in the conditional form of the verb. Although not mentioned, *agar* (if) is implied.

*tō* is also used to mean a different type of emphasis.

मैं तो नहीं जाऊंगा। I will not go.
*maiñ tō nahīñ jāūñgā*

यह काम तो मैं नहीं करूंगा। I will not do this job.
*yah kām tō maiñ nahīñ karūñgā*

रोटी तो मैं नहीं खाऊंगा। I will not eat bread.
*rōtī tō maiñ nahīñ khāuñgā*

In the first sentence the emphasis is on *maiñ,* meaning whoever might go, I shall not go. In the second sentence the emphasis is on *kām,* meaning whatever I do, I shall not do this particular work. In the third sentence, the emphasis is on *rōṭī* meaning I shall eat anything else, but not *rōṭī.*

**Changing verbs into Present Perfect or Past Perfect**

If the root of a verb end in *ī, ā* or any other vowel, add *yā, yī,* or *yē* to it to form the present perfect or past perfect.

**Examples :**

| | | | | |
|---|---|---|---|---|
| जा | *jā* | will be | गया | *gayā* |
| आ | *ā* | will be | आया | *āyā* |
| खा | *khā* | will be | खाया | *khāyā* |
| पी | *pī* | will be | पिया | *piyā* |
| सो | *sō* | will be | सोया | *sōyā* |

When the root of the verb ends in a consonant, the symbol of *ā* (ा) is added to it :

**Examples :**

| | | | | |
|---|---|---|---|---|
| लग | *lag* | will be | लगा | *lagā* |
| काट | *kāṭ* | will be | काटा | *kāṭā* |
| देख | *dēkh* | will be | देखा | *dēkhā* |
| सुन | *sun* | will be | सुना | *sunā* |

## Reading Exercise II

राम – नमस्ते। आप कैसी हैं ?

*Rām – namastē āp kaisī haiñ.*

सीता – मैं ठीक हूं, धन्यवाद, और आप कैसे हैं ?

*Sītā – maiñ ṭhīk huñ, dhanyavād, aur āp kaisē haiñ ?*

राम – मैं भी ठीक हूं। आपके पति कहां हैं ?

*Rām – maiñ bhī ṭhīk hūñ. āpkē pati kahāñ haiñ ?*

सीता – मेरे पति आगरा में है।

*Sītā – mērē pati Āgrā mēñ haiñ*

राम -- आपका घर कहां हैं ?

*Rām – āpkā ghar kahāñ hai ?*

सीता – मेरा घर हौज़खास में है।

*Sītā – mērā ghar Hauz Khās mēñ hai.*

राम – आपके कितने बच्चे हैं ?

*Rām – āpkē kitnē bachchē haiñ ?*

सीता – मेरे चार बच्चे हैं–दो बेटे और दो बेटियां।

*Sītā – mērē chār bachchē haiñ–dō bētē aur dō bētiyāñ*

राम – बच्चों के नाम क्या हैं ?

*Rām – bachchōñ kē nām kyā haiñ ?*

सीता – लड़को के नाम लव और कुश हैं।

*Sītā – laḍkōñ kē nām Lav aur Kush haiñ.*

राम – और लड़कियों के नाम ?

*Rām – aur laḍkiyōñ kē nām ?*

सीता – लड़कियों के नाम गीता और रीता हैं।

*Sītā – laḍkiyōñ kē nām Gītā or Rītā haiñ.*

राम – बहुत सुन्दर नाम है। आपका घर बड़ा है ?

*Rām – bahut sundar nām haiñ. āpkā ghar baḍa hai ?*

सीता – घर छोटा है लेकिन बाग बड़ा है।

*Sītā – ghar chhōṭā hai lēkin bāg baḍā hai.*

राम – कितने कमरे हैं ?

*Rām – kitānē kamarē haiñ ?*

सीता – चार कमरे हैं, एक बैठने-खाने का कमरा, और तीन सोने के कमरे।

*Sītā – chār kamarē haiñ, ēk baiṭhnē-khānē kā kamrā, aur tīn sōnē kē kamrē.*

राम – आप चाय लेंगी या कुछ ठंडा ?

*Rām – āp chāē lēñgī yā kuchchh ṭhandā ?*

सीता – सिर्फ़ ठंडा पानी चाहिए।

*Sītā – sirf ṭhandā pānī chāhiyē.*

राम – आप फल खाइए। केले बहुत मीठे हैं।

*Rām – āp phal khāiyē. kēlē bahut mīṭhē haiñ*

सीता – आपकी पत्नी और बच्चे कहां हैं ?

*Sītā – āpkī patnī aur bachchē kahāñ haiñ ?*

राम – बच्चे स्कूल में हैं। पत्नी रसोई में है।

*Rām – bachchē skūl mēñ haiñ. Patnī rasōī mēñ hai.*

**English translation of the text**

Ram – Namaste. How are you ?

Sita – I am all right, thank you, and how are you ?

Ram – I am all right, too. Where is your husband.

Sita – My husband is in Agra.

Ram – Where is your house ?

Sita – My house is in Hauz Khas.

| | | |
|---|---|---|
| Ram | – | How many children have you ? |
| Sita | – | I have four children–two sons and two daughters. |
| Ram | – | What are the children's names ? |
| Sita | – | Boys' names are Lav and Kush. |
| Ram | – | And the girls' names ? |
| Sita | – | Girls' names are Gīta and Rīta. |
| Ram | – | The names are very pretty. Is your house big ? |
| Sita | – | The house is small, but the garden is big. |
| Ram | – | How many rooms are there ? |
| Sita | – | There are four rooms. One sitting-dining room, and three bedrooms. |
| Ram | – | Will you have tea or something cold ? |
| Sita | – | I want only cold water. |
| Ram | – | Please eat the fruit. The bananas are very sweet. |
| Sita | – | Where are your wife and children ? |
| Ram | – | Children are in the school, wife is in the kitchen. |

**New words**

| | |
|---|---|
| *kaisī* | how |
| *dhanyavād* | thank you |
| *āpkē* | your |
| *pati* | husband |
| *mēñ* | in |
| *kitnē* | how many |
| *chār* | four |
| *dō* | two |
| *kyā* | what |
| *baithnē-khānē kā kamrā* | sitting-dining room |
| *sonē kā kamrā* | bedroom |

| | |
|---|---|
| *chāē* | tea |
| *kuchh* | some, something |
| *ṭhanḍā* | cold |
| *sirf* | only |
| *chāhiyē* | need, want |
| *khāiyē* | please eat |
| *mīṭhē* | sweet |
| *patnī* | wife |
| *skūl* | school |
| *rasōī* | kitchen |

* It would be noticed that *pati* and *patnī*, though third person singular, have been treated as plural. As has been explained in detail in the chapter on verbs, in the second or third person singular, the plural form is used for politeness.

* *Mērē chār bachchē haiñ* means, I have four children. Translated literally it would mean *mine four children are.* Translating literally explains how a sentence is constructed in Hindi. Since forms of expression vary from language to language, a literal translation from English into Hindi may become a bizzare expression in Hindi and vice versa. It is important, therefore, to know the forms of expressions that are peculiar to the language you are learning. Otherwise you may be able to make yourself understood all right but you will not be speaking the correct language.

* Also note the sentence *mujhkō ṭhanḍā pānī chāhiyē* (I want cold water). Translated literally it would be *maiñ ṭhanḍā pānī chāhtā hūn,* but the passive form is more common, Translated literally it would mean *to me cold water is needed.*

**Reading Exercise III**

भारत बहुत बड़ा देश है। यह बहुत प्राचीन देश है।

*Bhārat bahut baḍā dēsh hai. yah bahut prāchīn dēsh hai.*

इसके उत्तर में हिमालय पहाड़ है। दक्षिण में हिंद महासागर है।

*iskē uttar mēñ himālaya pahāḍ hai. dakshin mēñ Hind Mahāsāgar hai.*

पूर्व में बंगाल की खाड़ी है। पश्चिम में अरब महासागर है।

*pūrva mēñ Bangal kī khāḍī hai. paschim mēñ Arab Mahāsagar hai.*

गंगा सबसे बड़ी और पवित्र नदी है।

*Gangā sabsē baḍi aur pavitra nadī hai.*

भारत में कई बड़ी नदियां हैं।

*Bhārat mēñ kaī baḍi nadiyāñ haiñ.*

भारत की राजधानी नयी दिल्ली है।

*Bhārat kī rājdhānī Naī Dillī hai.*

दिल्ली सुन्दर नगर है।

*Dillī sundar nagar hai.*

दूसरे बड़े नगर बंबई, कलकत्ता और मद्रास हैं।

*dūsarē baḍē nagar Bambaī, Kalkattā aur Madrās haiñ.*

भारत की आबादी बहुत ज़्यादा है।

*Bhārat kī ābādī bahut zyādā hai.*

**Translation into English**

India (Bharat) is a very big country. It is an ancient country. In the north are the Himalaya mountain ranges. In the south is the Indian Ocean. In the east is the Bay of Bengal. In the west is the Arabian Sea. The Ganges is the biggest and the holiest river. There are several big rivers in India. New

Delhi is the capital of India. Delhi is a beautiful city. Other big cities are Bombay, Calcutta and Madras. There is over population in India.

**New words**

| | |
|---|---|
| *bahut* | very |
| *dēsh* | country |
| *prāchīn* | ancient |
| *uttar* | north |
| *pahāḍ* | mountain |
| *dakshiñ* | south |
| *pūrva* | east |
| *pashchim* | west |
| *pavitra* | holy |
| *nadī* | river |
| *kaī* | several |
| *rājdhānī* | capital |
| *nagar* | city |
| *dūsarē* | other |
| *ābādi* | population |
| *bahut zyādā* | very much, too much |

**Reading Exercise IV**

मैं नयी दिल्ली में रहता हूं। मेरा भाई पुरानी दिल्ली में रहता है। मेरी बहिन बम्बई में हैं। वह साल में एक बार दिल्ली आती है। उसके पति और बच्चे भी आते हैं। मेरा दफ्तर पुरानी दिल्ली में है। मैं हर रोज़ बस से आता-जाता हूं। हम लोग बंगाली हैं। मेरे माता-पिता कलकत्ता में रहते हैं। आपने कलकत्ता देखा है ? मुझको कलकत्ता बहुत पसंद है। मुझको दिल्ली भी पसंद है। आप दक्षिण के हैं ? आपकी पत्नी हिन्दी बोलती है ?

मेरी पत्नी हिन्दी कुछ-कुछ बोलती है। मेरे बच्चे अच्छी हिन्दी बोलते हैं। आप लोग बंगला समझते हैं ?

*maiñ naī Dillī mēñ rahtā ḥūñ. mērā bhaī purānī Dillī mēñ rahtā hai. mērī bahin Bambaī mēñ hai. vah sāl mēñ ēk bār Dillī ātī hai. uskē pati ōr bachchē bhī ātē haiñ. mēra daftar purāni Dillí mēñ hai. maiñ har rōz bas sē ātā-jātā hūñ. ham lōg Bangālī haiñ. mērē matā-pitā Kalkattā mēñ rahtē haiñ. āpnē Kalkattā dēkhā hai ? āp dakshin kē haiñ ? āpkī patnī Hindī bōltī hai ? mērī patnī Hindī kuchh-kuchh bōltī hai. mērē bachchē-achchhī Ḥindi bōltē haiñ. āp lōg Banglā samajhtē haiñ ?*

I live in New Delhi. My brother lives in Old Delhi. My sister lives in Bombay. She comes to Delhi once in a year. Her husband and children come too. My office is in Old Delhi. Everyday I come and go by bus. We are Bengalis. My mother and father live in Calcutta. Have you seen Calcutta ? I like Calcutta very much. I like Delhi too. Are you from the South ? Does your wife speak Hindi ? My wife speaks a little Hindi. My children speak good Hindi. Do you understand Bangla (Bengali) ?

**New words**

| | |
|---|---|
| *rahtā hūñ* | live |
| *bhāī* | brother |
| *daftar* | ofiice |
| *shahar* | city |
| *mujhkō pasand hai* | I like it |
| *bhī* | also, too |
| *dakshin* | south |
| *patnī* | wife |

| | |
|---|---|
| *Bañglā* | language of Bengal |
| *samajhte haiñ* | do they understand ? |
| *har* | every |
| *rōz* | day |
| *ātā-jātā* | come and go |
| *apnē* | my |
| *parivār* | family |
| *ke sāth* | with |
| *itwār* | Sunday |
| *dēkhā hai ?* | have you seen ? |

**Reading Exercise V**

राम – नमस्ते।

Rām – *namastē*

डिक – नमस्ते।

Dick – *namastē*

राम – आपका शुभ नाम ?

Rām – *āpkā shubh nām ?*

डिक – मेरा नाम डिक ब्राउन है।

Dick – *mērā nām Dick Brown hai*

राम – आप भारत में कब से हैं ?

Rām – *āp Bhārat mēñ kab sē haiñ ?*

डिक – चार महीने से।

Dick – *chār mahīnē sē.*

राम – आप कहां रहते हैं ?

Rām – *āp kahān rahtē haiñ ?*

डिक – अभी तो मैं होटल में रहता हूं।

Dick – *abhī tō maiñ hōṭal mēñ rahtā hūñ.*

राम – किस होटल में ?
Rām – *kis hōṭal mēñ ?*

डिक – जनपथ होटल में
Dick – *Janpath hōṭal mēñ.*

राम – अच्छा होटल है ?
Rām – *achchhā hōṭal hai ?*

डिक – काफी अच्छा है।
Dick – *kāfī achchhā hai.*

राम – आप विवाहित हैं ?
Rām – *āp vivāhit hai ?*

डिक – जी हां, मेरे दो बच्चे भी हैं।
Dick – *jī hāñ, mērē dō bachchē bhī haiñ.*

राम – वे कहां हैं ?
Rām – *vē kahāñ haiñ ?*

डिक – अभी तो वे अमरीका में हैं।
Dick – *abhī tō vē Amirkā mēñ haiñ.*

राम – वे भारत नहीं आएंगे ?
Rām – *vē Bhārat nahīñ āyēñgē ?*

डिक – ज़रूर आएंगे, जब मुझको घर मिलेगा।
Dick – *zarūr āyēñgē, jab mujhkō ghar milēgā.*

राम – आपको घर कहां चाहिए ?
Rām – *āpkō ghar kahāñ chāhiyē ?*

डिक – सुन्दर नगर, जोरबाग, कहीं भी।
Dick – *Sundar Nagar, Jorbāg, kahīñ bhī.*

राम – कैसा घर चाहिए ?
Rām – *kaisā ghar chāhiyē ?*

डिक – कम-से-कम पांच कमरे होने चाहिए। नौकरों के लिए भी कमरे होने चाहिए।

Dick – *kam-sē-kam pāñch kamrē hōnē chāhiē. naukarōñ kē liyē bhī kamrē hōnē chāhiyē.*

राम – शायद मैं आपकी मदद कर सकूं।

Rām – *shāyad maiñ āpkī madad kar sakūñ.*

डिक – बड़ी मेहरबानी होगी। लेकिन मैं आपको तकलीफ़ नहीं देना चाहता।

Dick – *barī meharbānī hōgī. lēkin maiñ āpkō taklīf nahiñ dēnā chāhtā.*

राम – तकलीफ़ की कोई बात नहीं।

Rām – *taklīf kī kōī bāt nahiñ.*

डिक – अच्छी बात है। आपको कोई अच्छा घर मालूम है ?

Dick – *achchhī bāt hai. āpkō kōī achchhā ghar mālūm hai ?*

राम – मैं आपको अपने साथ ले चलूँगा। दो-चार घर दिखाऊंगा।

Rām – *maiñ āpkō apnē sāth lē chalūñgā. do-chār ghar dikhaūñgā.*

**English translation**

Ram – Namaste.

Dick – Namaste.

Ram – What is your name, please ?

Dick – My name is Dick Brown.

Ram – How long have you been in India ?

Dick – For four monts.

Ram – Where do you live ?

Dick – At the moment I am staying in a hotel.

Ram – In which hotel ?

Dick – In Janpath Hotel.
Ram – Is it a good hotel ?
Dick – It is quite good.
Ram – Are you married ?
Dick – Yes. I have two children.
Ram – Where are they ?
Dick – At the moment they are in America.
Ram – Won't they come to India ?
Dick – They certainly will come, when I get a house.
Ram – Where do you want the house ?
Dick – Sundar Nagar, Jorbag, anywhere.
Ram – What sort of a house do you want ?
Dick – There should be at least five rooms. There should be rooms for servants too.
Ram – May be I can help you.
Dick – That will be very kind. But I don't want to trouble you.
Rām – There is no trouble at all.
Dick – Okay then. Do you know of any good house ?
Ram – I shall take you with me.
(I shall) show you a few houses.

**New words**

| | |
|---|---|
| *kab sē* | since when |
| *vivāhit* | married |
| *abhī tō* | at the moment |
| *kaisā* | what sort of |
| *kam-sē-kam* | minimum, at least |
| *shāyad* | perhaps |
| *taklīf (f)* | trouble |

| | |
|---|---|
| *mālūm* | known |
| *dō-chār* | idiomatic way of saying a few |

**Reading Exercise VI**

बरसात *barsāt*

गरमी के बाद बरसात आती है।
*garmī kē bād barsāt ātī hai.*

बरसात जुलाई से सितम्बर तक रहती है।
*barsāt July sē Sitambar tak rahtī hai.*

बरसात का मौसम स्वास्थ्य के लिए अच्छा नहीं है।
*barsāt kā māusam svāsthya kē liyē achchhā nahīñ hai.*

बीमारियां फैलती हैं।
*bīmāriyāñ phailatī haiñ.*

मक्खी-मच्छर बहुत परेशान करते हैं।
*makkhī-machchar bahut parēshān kartē haiñ.*

कीड़े-मकोड़े भी बहुत ज्यादा हो जाते हैं।
*kīḍē-makōḍē bhī bahut zyādā hō jātē haiñ.*

अच्छी सब्ज़ी-तरकारी भी नहीं मिलती।
*achchhī sabzi-tarkārī bhī nahīñ milatī.*

सड़कों पर पानी भर जाता है।
*saḍkōn par pānī bhar jātā hai.*

लेकिन बरसात बहुत ज़रूरी भी तो है।
*lēkin barsāt bahut zarūrī bhī tō hai.*

बारिश की पहली बौछार कितनी अच्छी लगती है !
*bārish kī pahlī bauchhār kitnī achchhī lagtī hai !*

लोग चैन की सांस लेते हैं।
*lōg chain kī sāñs lētē haiñ.*

बच्चे पेड़ों से अमरूद और जामुन तोड़ कर खाते हैं।
*bachchē pēḍōñ sē amrūd aur jāmun tōḍ kar khātē haiñ.*

बरसात में खाने-पीने में बहुत सावधान रहना चाहिए।
*barsāt mēñ khānē-pīnē mēñ bahut sāvdhān rahnā chāhivē.*

बाज़ार की चीज़ें नहीं खानी चाहिए।
*bāzār kī chīzēñ nahīñ khānī chāhiyē.*

उबला पानी पीना चाहिए।
*ublā pānī pīnā chāhiyē.*

**English translation**

**The rainy season**

The rainy season comes after summer.
The rainy season lasts from July to September.
The rainy season is not good for health.
Diseases spread.
Flies and mosquitoes annoy a lot.
There are too many insects, too.
Good vegetables are not available.
Roads are full of water.
But the rain is also very essential.
How pleasant are the first showers of rain !
People have a sigh of relief.
Children pluck guavas and rose apples from trees to eat.
One should be very careful about what one eats and drinks in the rainy season.
One should not eat in the bazar.
One should drink boiled water.

**New words**

| | |
|---|---|
| *kē bād* | after |
| *sē* | from |
| *tak* | upto |
| *svāsthya* | health |
| *phailitī haiñ* | spread |
| *makkhī* | flies |
| *machchhar* | mosquitoes |

(मक्खी-मच्छर are often used as a compound word to mean both)

| | |
|---|---|
| *kīḍē* | insects |
| *makōḍē* | spiders |
| (Note : the compound word *kīḍē-makōḍē*) | |
| *sabzi* | green vegetables |
| *tarkārī* | a general term for vegetables |
| *bhar jātā hai* | gets filled |
| *zarūrī* | essential |
| *pahlī* | first |
| *bauchhār* | showers |
| *kitanī* | how much |
| *chain* | relief |
| *sāñs* | breath |
| *amrūd* | guava |
| *jāmun* | rose apple |
| *tōḍ kar* | pluck |
| *khānā-pīnā* | eating-drinking |
| *ubālā* (int. v) | boiled |

## Reading Exercise VII

| | | |
|---|---|---|
| गोपाल | – | आप राम को जानते हैं ? |
| Gōpāl | – | *āp Rām kō jāntē haiñ ?* |
| हरी | – | जी नहीं, मैं नहीं जानता। |
| Harī | – | *jī nahīñ, maiñ nahīñ jāntā.* |
| गोपाल | – | वह आपके पड़ोस में रहता है। |
| Gōpāl | – | *vah āpkē paḍōs mēñ rahtā hai.* |
| हरी | – | मुझको अफसोस है कि मैं उससे कभी नहीं मिला। |
| Harī | – | *mujhkō afsōs hai ki maiñ ussē kabhī nahī milā.* |
| गोपाल | – | आप उससे जरूर मिलिए। वह मेरा दोस्त है। |
| Gōpāl | – | *āp ussē zarūr miliyē. vah mērā dost hai.* |
| हरी | – | ज़रूर मिलूंगा। |
| Harī | – | *zarūr milūñgā.* |
| गोपाल | – | राम बहुत दिलचस्प आदमी है। |
| Gōpāl | – | *Rām bahut dilchasp ādmī hai.* |
| हरी | – | बहुत अच्छी बात है। |
| Harī | – | *bahut achchhī bāt hai.* |
| गोपाल | – | मैं राम को पिछले पन्द्रह सालों से जानता हूं। |
| Gōpāl | – | *maiñ Rām ko pichhlē pandrah sālōñ sē jāntā hūñ.* |
| हरी | – | क्या आप साथ-साथ पढ़ते थे ? |
| Hari | – | *kyā āp sāth-sāth paḍhtē thē ?* |
| गोपाल | – | जी हां, हम एक ही कालिज में पढ़ते थे। |
| Gōpāl | – | *jī hāñ, ham ēk hī kalij mēñ paḍhtē thē.* |
| हरी | – | कृपा कर के उनका पता दीजिए। उनके मकान का नंबर क्या है ? |
| Harī | – | *kripā kar kē unkā patā dījiyē. unkē makān kā nambar kyā hai ?* |

गोपाल – नंबर तो मुझको याद नहीं है।

Gōpāl – *nambar tō mujhkō yād nahīñ hai.*

हरी – अच्छा, कल बता दीजिए।

Harī – *achchhā, kal batā dījiyē.*

गोपाल – उसका बड़ा-सा सफेद मकान है। उसके दरवाजे पर पीपल का पेड़ है।

Gōpāl – *uskā baḍā-sā safēd makān hai. uskē darvāzē par pipal kā pēḍ hai.*

हरी – मैं ढूँढ़ने की कोशिश करूंगा।

Harī – *maiñ dhūñdhnē kī kōshish karūñgā.*

गोपाल – उसके घर का फाटक हरा है।

Gōpāl – *uskē ghar kā phātak harā hai.*

हरी – अच्छा, याद रखूंगा। आप भी मेरे साथ चलिए।

Harī – *achchhā, yād rakhūñgā. āp bhī mērē sāth chaliyē.*

गोपाल – हां, यह ठीक है। चलिए, मैं आपके साथ चलता हूं।

Gōpāl – *hāñ, yah ṭhīk hai. Chaliyē maiñ āpkē sāth chaltā hūñ.*

**English Translation**

Gopal – Do you know Ram ?

Hari – No, I don't know.

Gopal – He lives in your neighbourhood.

Hari – I am sorry that I have never met him.

Gopal – Do meet him. He is my friend.

Hari – I shall definitely meet him.

Gopal – Ram is a very interesting man.

Hari – That's very good.

Gopal – I have known Ram for the last fifteen years.

Hari – Did you study together ?

Gopal – Yes, we studied in the same college.

Hari – Please give me his address. What is his house number ?

Gopal – I don't remember the number.

Hari – Okay, tell me tomorrow.

Gopal – His is a big and white house. There is a pipal tree at the gate.

Hari – I shall try to locate it.

Gopal – The gate of his house is green.

Hari – Okay, I shall remember it. You come with me too.

Gopal – That is right. Come, I shall come with you.

## New words

| | |
|---|---|
| *paḍōs* | neighbourhood |
| *jāntē haiñ ?* | do you know ? |
| *mujhkō afsōs hai* | I am sorry |
| *kabhī nahīñ* | never |
| *milā* | met |
| *dōst* | friend |
| *dilchasp* | interesting |
| *pichhlē* | last (bygone) |
| *sālōñ* | years |
| *sāth-sāth* | together |
| *ēk hī* | the same |
| *kripā kar kē* | please, kindly |
| *patā* | address |
| *dījiyē* | give |

| | |
|---|---|
| *yād nahīñ hai* | don't remember |
| *batā* | tell |
| *pīpal* | a kind of tree |
| *dhūñdhnā* | search for |
| *kōshish karūñgā* | shall try |
| *phāṭak* | gate |
| *yād rakhūñgā* | shall remember |
| *mērē sāth* | with me |

**Reading Exercise VIII**

हरी – आप कहां गये थे ?
Harī – *āp kahāñ gayē thē ?*
गोपाल – मैं बाज़ार गया था ।
Gōpāl – *maiñ bāzār gayā thā.*
हरी – आप कैसे गये थे ? गाड़ी से ?
Harī – *āp kaisē gayē thē ? Gaḍī sē ?*
गोपाल – जी नहीं, मैं बस से गया था ।
Gōpāl – *jī nahīñ, maiñ bas sē gayā thā.*
हरी – आपकी गाड़ी कहां है ?
Harī – *āpkī gāḍī kahāñ hai ?*
गोपाल – गाड़ी खराब है, इसलिये मैं बस से गया ।
Gōpāl – *ġaḍī kharāb hai isliyē maiñ bas sē gayā.*
हरी – आज दुकाने खुली हैं ?
Harī – *āj dūkānēñ khulī haiñ ?*
गोपाल – जी हां, सब दुकानें खुली हैं ।
Gōpāl – *jī hāñ, sab dukānē khulīn haiñ.*
हरी – मुझको परदे का कपड़ा खरीदना है ।
Harī – *mujhkō pardē kā kapḍā kharīdanā hai.*

गोपाल – बाजार मेरे घर के पीछे ही है।
Gōpāl – *bāzār mērē ghar kē pīchhē hī hai.*

हरी – तो फिर आप बस में क्यों गये थे ?
Harī – *tō phir āp bas mēñ kyoñ gayē thē ?*

गोपाल – मैं तो सब्ज़ी मंडी गया था।
Gōpāl – *maiñ tō subzī mandī gayā thā.*

हरी – मेरे घर के सामने बाग है।
Harī – *mērē ghar kē samnē bāgh hai.*

गोपाल – शाम को बाग में बच्चे खेलते हैं।
Gōpāl – *shām kō bāgh mēñ bachchē kheltē haiñ.*

हरी – मेरे बच्चे घर के अन्दर ही खेलते हैं।
Harī – *mērē bachchē ghar kē andar hī kheltē haiñ.*

गोपाल – उनको बाग में खेलना पसन्द नहीं है ?
Gōpāl – *unkō bāgh mēñ khelnā pasand nahīñ hai ?*

हरी – जी नहीं। अपने बच्चों को मेरे घर भेजिये।
Harī – *jī nahīñ apnē bachchōñ kō mērē ghar bhejiyē.*

गोपाल – मैं आया तो बाहर का दरवाजा खुला था।
Gōpāl – *maiñ āyā tō bāhar kā darvāzā khulā thā.*

हरी – किसने खोला ?
Harī – *kisnē khōlā ?*

गोपाल – मैं नहीं जानता। शायद नौकर ने खुला छोड़ दिया था।
Gōpāl – *maiñ nahīñ jāntā. shāyad naukar nē khulā chhoḍ diyā thā.*

हरी – नौकर बहुत लापरवाह है।
Harī – *naukar bahut lāparvāh hai.*

गोपाल – आजकल बहुत चोरियां होती हैं।

Gōpāl – *ājkal bahut chōriyāñ hōtī haiñ.*

हरी – लेकिन मेरा नौकर बिल्कुल नहीं समझता।

Harī – *lēkin mērā naukar bilkul nahīñ samajhtā.*

**New Words**

| | |
|---|---|
| *gāḍī* | car |
| *khulī* | open |
| *pardē kā kapḍā* | curtain material |
| *ghar kē pīchhē* | behind the house |
| *sabzī mandī* | wholesale vegetable market |
| *sāmnē* | in front |
| *khēltē haiñ* | play |
| *andar* | inside |
| *bhējiyē* | send |
| *lāparvāh* | careless |
| *chōriyāñ* | thefts |
| *samajhtā* | understand |

**Reading Exercise IX**

यह गुलाब लाल है। इसकी पत्तियाँ हरी हैं। मेरे बाग में कई रंग के गुलाब हैं–पीले, गुलाबी, सफेद और लाल। मेरे बाग में फल के भी बहुत पेड़ हैं। मेरा माली होशियार और मेहनती है। वह सारा दिन बाग में काम करता है। वह ईमानदार भी है। उसके कई छोटे-छोटे बच्चे हैं। वह काफ़ी गरीब है। उसकी पत्नी भी मेरे घर में काम करती है। वह कुछ-कुछ सुस्त है। माली के बच्चे बहुत दुबले-पतले हैं। अक्सर बीमार रहते हैं।

आजकल मौसम अच्छा नहीं है। बाजार में तरकारियाँ बहुत महँगी हैं। फल भी महँगे हैं। कोई चीज़ सस्ती नहीं है। माली के बच्चे समझदार है। बाज़ार की गंदी चीज़ें नहीं खाते।

*yah gulāb lāl hai. iskī pattiyāñ harī haiñ. mērē bāg mēñ kaī rang kē gulāb haiñ—pīlē, gulābī, safed aur lāl. mērē bāg mēñ phal kē bhī bahut pēḍ haiñ. mērā mālī hōshiyār aur mēhnatī hai. vah sārā din bāgh mēñ kām kartā hai. vah īmāndār bhī hai. uskē kaī chhōṭē-chhōṭē bachchē haiñ. vah kafi garīb hai. uskī patnī bhī mērē ghar mēñ kām kartī hai. vah kuchh-kuchh sust hai. mālī kē bachchē bahut dublē-patlē haiñ. aksar bīmār rahtē haiñ.*

*ājkal māusam achchhā nahīñ hai. bāzār mēñ tarakāriyāñ bahut mahañgī haiñ. phal bhī mahañgē haiñ. koī chīz sastī nahīñ hai. mālī kē bachchē samajhdār haiñ. bāzār kī gandī chīzēñ nahīñ khātē.*

**New Words**

| | |
|---|---|
| *gulāb* | rose |
| *lāl* | red |
| *harī* | green |
| *pattiyāñ* | leaves |
| *pīlē* | yellow |
| *gulābī* | pink |
| *safēd* | white |
| *bahut* | many |
| *pēḍ* | tree |
| *mālī* | gardener |
| *hōshiyār* | intelligent, competent |
| *mēhnatī* | hard working |
| *kaī* | several |
| *chhōtē-chhōṭē* | small-small |
| *kāfi* | quite |
| *garīb* | poor |
| *kām kartī hai* | works |

| | |
|---|---|
| *dublē-patalē* | lean and thin |
| *aksar* | often |
| *tarakāriyāñ* | vegetables |
| *mahañgē* | expensive |
| *gandī* | dirty, unclean |
| *nahīñ khātē* | don't eat |
| *chīzēñ* | things |
| *sastē* | cheap |
| *samajhdār* | sensible |

CHAPTER NINE

# A MINIMAL DICTIONARY

**Greetings**–अभिवादन

| | | |
|---|---|---|
| Good Morning, | नमस्ते, | *namastē,* |
| Good Evening, | नमस्कार | *namaskār* |
| Good Night | | |

**Time**–समय

| | | |
|---|---|---|
| day | दिन | *din* (m) |
| morning | सवेरा | *savērā* (m) |
| afternoon | दोपहर | *dōpahar* (f) |
| evening | शाम | *shām* (f) |
| night | रात | *rāt* (f) |
| week | हफ़्ता, सप्ताह | *haftā, saptāh* (m) |
| fortnight | पखवाड़ा | *pakhwāḍā* (m) |
| month | महीना, मास | *mahinā, mās* (m) |
| year | साल, वर्ष | *sāl, varsh* (m) |
| decade | दशक | *dashak* (m) |
| century | सदी, शताब्दी | *sadī, shatābdī* (f). |
| today | आज | *āj* (m) |
| yesterday | कल | *kal* (m) |
| tomorrow | कल | *kal* (m) |
| the day before yesterday | | परसों *parsōñ* (m) |
| the day after tomorrow | | परसों *parsōñ* (m) |

**Numbers**—गिनती

| | | |
|---|---|---|
| one | एक | *ēk* |
| two | दो | *dō* |
| three | तीन | *tīn* |
| four | चार | *chār* |
| five | पाँच | *pāñch* |
| six | छे: | *chhē* |
| seven | सात | *sāt* |
| eight | आठ | *āṭh* |
| nine | नौ | *nau* |
| ten | दस | *das* |
| eleven | ग्यारह | *gyārah* |
| twelve | बारह | *bārah* |
| thirteen | तेरह | *tērah* |
| fourteen | चौदह | *chaudah* |
| fifteen | पंद्रह | *pandrah* |
| sixteen | सोलह | *sōlah* |
| seventeen | सत्रह | *satrah* |
| eighteen | अठारह | *aṭhārah* |
| nineteen | उन्नीस | *unnīs* |
| twenty | बीस | *bīs* |
| hundred | सौ | *sau* |
| thousand | हज़ार | *hazār* |

**Ordinal numbers**—अनुक्रम संख्या

| | | |
|---|---|---|
| first | पहला | *pahlā* |
| second | दूसरा | *dūsarā* |
| third | तीसरा | *tīsarā* |
| fourth | चौथा | *chauthā* |

| | | |
|---|---|---|
| fifth | पांचवां | *pāñchvāñ* |
| sixth | छठा | *chhaṭhā* |
| seventh | सातवां | *sātvāñ* |
| eighth | आठवां | *āṭhvāñ* |
| ninth | नौवां | *nauvāñ* |
| tenth | दसवां | *dasvāñ* |
| eleventh | ग्यारहवां | *gyārahvañ* |
| twelfth | वारहवां | *bārahvāñ* |
| thirteenth | तेरहवां | *tērahvāñ* |
| fourteenth | चौदहवां | *chaudahvāñ* |
| fifteenth | पंद्रहवां | *pandrahvāñ* |
| sixteenth | सोलहवां | *sōlvhāñ* |
| seventeenth | सत्रहवां | *satravhāñ* |
| eighteenth | अठारहवां | *aṭhārhvāñ* |
| nineteenth | उन्नीसवां | *unnīsvāñ* |
| twentieth | वीसवां | *bīsvāñ* |
| hundredth | सौवां | *sauvāñ* |
| thousandth | हजारवां | *hazārvāñ* |
| dozen | दर्जन | *darjan* |
| half-a-dozen | आधा दर्जन | *ādhā darjan* |

**Planets—ग्रह**

| | | |
|---|---|---|
| Sun | सूर्य | *sūrya* |
| Moon | चन्द्र | *chandra* |
| Mars | मंगल | *mangal* |
| Mercury | बुध | *budh* |
| Jupiter | वृहस्पति | *brihaspati* |
| Venus | शुक्र | *shukra* |
| Saturn | शनि | *shani* |

**Days of the week–सप्ताह के दिन**

| | | |
|---|---|---|
| day of the week | वार | *vār* (m) |
| Sunday | इतवार | *itvār* or *ravivar* |
| Monday | सोमवार | *sōmvār* |
| Tuesday | मंगलवार | *mangalvār* |
| Wednesday | बुधवार | *budhvār* |
| Thursday | बृहस्पतिवार | *brihaspativār* (also called vīrvār) |
| Friday | शुक्रवार | *shukravār* |
| Saturday | शनिवार | *shanivār* (also called *shanīchar*) |

**Directions–दिशाएं**

| | | |
|---|---|---|
| direction | दिशा | *dishā* (f) |
| east | पूर्व | *pūrva* (m) |
| west | पश्चिम | *pashchim* (m) |
| north | उत्तर | *uttar* (m) |
| south | दक्षिण | *dakshin* (m) |

**Human body–मानव शरीर**

| | | |
|---|---|---|
| ankle | टखना | *takhanā* (m) |
| arm | बांह, बांजू | *bāñh, bājū* (f) |
| armpit | बगल | *bagal* (f) |
| back | पीठ | *pīṭh* (f) |
| beard | दाढ़ी | *dāḍhi* (f) |
| blood | खून | *khūn* (m) |
| body | शरीर | *sharīr* (m) |
| bone | हड्डी | *haḍḍī* (f) |

| | | |
|---|---|---|
| brain | दिमाग | *dimāg* (m) |
| breast (woman's) | स्तन | *stan* (m) |
| cheek | गाल | *gāl* (m) |
| chest | छाती | *chhātī* (f) |
| chin | ठोड़ी | *ṭhōḍī* (f) |
| ear | कान | *kān* (m) |
| elbow | कोहनी | *kōhnī* (f) |
| eye | आँख | *āñkh* (f) |
| eyeball | पुतली | *putlī* (f) |
| eyebrow | भौं | *bhāūñ* (f) |
| eyelashes | पलक | *palak* (f) |
| face | चेहरा | *chēhrā* (m) |
| finger | अंगुली | *añgulī* (f) |
| finger-nail | नाखून | *nākhūn* (f) |
| flesh | मांस | *māñs* (m) |
| foot | पैर | *pair* (m) |
| forehead | माथा | *māthā* (m) |
| hand | हाथ | *hāth* (m) |
| head | सिर | *sir* (m) |
| heart | दिल, हृदय | *dil, hridaya* (m) |
| hair | बाल | *bāl* (m) |
| heel | एड़ी | *ēḍī* (f) |
| kidney | गुर्दा | *gurdā* (m) |
| lip | होठ | *hōṭh* (m) |
| liver | जिगर | *jigar* (m) |
| lung | फेफड़ा | *phēphaḍā* (m) |
| moustache | मूंछ | *mūñchh* (f) |
| mouth | मुँह | *mūñh* (m) |
| neck | गर्दन | *gardan* (f) |

| | | |
|---|---|---|
| nail | नाखून | *nākhūn* (m) |
| nose | नाक | *nāk* (f) |
| palm | हथेली | *hathēlī* (f) |
| shoulder | कंधा | *kandhā* (m) |
| skin | चमड़ी | *chamḍī* (f) |
| skull | खोपड़ी | *khopḍī* (f) |
| spine | रीढ़ | *rīḍh* (f) |
| stomach | पेट | *pēṭ* (m) |
| teeth | दांत | *dāñt* (m) |
| thigh | जांघ | *jāñgh* (f) |
| throat | गला | *galā* (m) |
| thumb | अंगूठा | *añguṭhā* (m) |
| toe | पैर की अंगुली | *pair-kī-añgulī* (f) |
| tongue | जीभ | *jībh* (f) |
| vein | नस | *nas* (f) |
| waist | कमर | *kamar* (f) |
| wrist | कलाई | *kalāī* (f) |

**Animals**–पशु

| | | |
|---|---|---|
| animal | जानवर, पशु | *jānvar* (m), pashu |
| bear | भालू | *bhālū* (m) |
| buffalo | भैंसा, भैंस | *bhaiñsā* (m), *bhaiñs* (f) |
| bullock | बैल | *bail* (m) |
| cat | बिल्ली | *billī* (f) |
| camel | ऊंट | *ūnṭ* (m), *ūnṭnī* (f) |
| cow | गाय | *gāy* (f) |
| calf | बछड़ा, बछिया | *bachhrā* (m), *bachhiā* (f) |
| deer | हिरन | *hiran* (m) |

| | | |
|---|---|---|
| dog | कुत्ता | *kuttā* (m) |
| bitch | कुतिया | *kutiā* (f) |
| donkey | गधा | *gadhā* (m) |
| elephant | हाथी | *hāthī* (m), *hathinī* (f) |
| fox | लोमड़ी | *lomaḍ* (m), *lōmḍī* (f) |
| goat | बकरी | *bakarā* (m), *bakarī* (f) |
| horse | घोड़ा | *ghoḍā* (m) |
| mare | घोड़ी | *ghoḍī* (f) |
| mule | खच्चर | *khachchar* |
| monkey | बंदर, बंदरिया | *bandar* (m), *bandariyā* (f) |
| mouse | चूहा | *chūhā* (m) *chuhiyā* (f) |
| lamb | मेमना | *mēmanā* (m & f). |
| leopard | तेंदुआ | *tēnduā* (m) |
| lion | सिंह, बब्बर शेर | *sinha, babbar shēr* (m) |
| lioness | सिंहनी | *sinhanī* (f) |
| python | अजगर | *ajgar* (m) |
| snake | सांप | *sāñp* (m) |
| sheep | भेड़ | *bhēḍ* (f) |
| skunk | छछूंदर | *chhac̄hhūndar* (m) |
| squirrel | गिलहरी | *gilahrī* (f) |
| tiger | शेर | *shēr* (m) |
| tigress | शेरनी | *shērnī* (f) |

**Birds—पक्षी**

| | | |
|---|---|---|
| bat | चमगादड़ | *chamgādaḍ* (m) |
| bird | पक्षी, चिड़िया | *pakshī, chiḍīyā* (f) |
| crow | कौवा | *kauvā* (m) |
| cock | मुर्गा | *murgā* (m) |

| | | |
|---|---|---|
| crane | सारस | *sāras* (m) |
| cuckoo | कोयल | *kōyal* (f) |
| duck | बत्तख | *battakh* (f) |
| hen | मुर्गी | *murgī* (f) |
| kite | चील | *chīl* (f) |
| nightingale | बुलबुल | *bulbul* (f) |
| owl | उल्लू | *ullū* (m) |
| partridge | तीतर | *tītar* (m) |
| parrot | तोता | *tōtā* (m) |
| peacock | मोर | *mōr* (m) |
| pigeon | कबूतर | *kabūtar* (m) |
| sparrow | गौरैया | *gauraiyā* (f) |
| swan | हंस | *hans* (m) |
| vulture | गिद्ध | *giddh* (m) |
| wolf | भेड़िया | *bhēḍyā* |

**Fish and marine animals**—मछली और जलचर

| | | |
|---|---|---|
| crab | केकड़ा | *kēkḍā* (m) |
| crocodile | मगरमच्छ | *magarmachchha* (m) |
| fish | मछली | *machhlī* (f) |
| tortoise | कछुआ | *kachhuā* (m) |

**Insects**—कीट

| | | |
|---|---|---|
| ant | चींटी | *chīñṭī* (f) |
| ant (white) | दीमक | *dīmak* (f) |
| bee | मधुमक्खी | *madhumakkhī* (f) |
| bug | खटमल | *khaṭamal* (m) |
| butterfly | तितली | *titalī* (f) |
| fly | मक्खी | *makkhī* (f) |

| | | |
|---|---|---|
| germs | कीटाणु | *kīṭānu* (m) |
| glow worm | जुगनू | *juganū* (m) |
| insect | कीड़ा | *kīḍā* (m) |
| lizard | छिपकली | *chhipkalī* (f) |
| locust | टिड्डी | *tiḍḍī* (f) |
| mosquito | मच्छर | *machchhar* (m) |
| scorpion | बिच्छू | *bichchhū* (m) |
| spider | मकड़ी | *makḍī* (f) |

**Foodstuff**–खाद्य पदार्थ

| | | |
|---|---|---|
| bread | रोटी, चपाती | *rōṭī* (f), *chapātī* (f) |
| butter | मक्खन | *makhan* (m) |
| butter-milk | छाछ | *chhāchh* (m) |
| cashewnut | काजू | *kājū* (m) |
| chicken | मुर्गी | *murgī* (f) |
| clarified butter | घी | *ghī* (m) |
| coconut (green) | नारियल | *nāriyal* (m) |
| coconut (dry) | खोपरा | *khōprā* (m) |
| coffee | कॉफी | *kaufī* (f) |
| cottage cheese | पनीर | *panīr* (m) |
| corn | मक्का | *makkā* (m) |
| curd | दही | *dahī* (m) |
| dates | खजूर | *khajūr* (m) |
| dry fruit | मेवा | *mēvā* (f) |
| egg | अंडा | *anḍā* (m) |
| fish | मछली | *machhlī* (f) |
| flour (whole wheat) | आटा | *ātā* (m) |
| flour (white) | मैदा | *maidā* (f) |
| gram | चना | *chanā (m)* |

| | | |
|---|---|---|
| jaggery | गुड़ | *guḍ* (m) |
| lentils | दाल | *dāl* (f) |
| milk | दूध | *dūdh* (m) |
| oil | तेल | *tēl* (m) |
| pickle | अचार | *achār* (m) |
| rice | चावल | *chāval* (m) |
| salt | नमक | *namak* (m) |
| sugar | चीनी | *chīnī* (f) |
| wheat | गेहूं | *gēhūñ* (m) |

**Vegetables**–सब्ज़ियाँ

| | | |
|---|---|---|
| beans (green) | सेम | *sēm* (f) |
| beans (string) | लोबिया | *lōbiyā* (f) |
| beans (French) | फरास बीन | *farās bīn* (f) |
| cabbage | बंदगोभी | *bandgōbhī* (f) |
| capsicum | शिमला मिर्च | *shimlā mirch* (f) |
| carrot | गाजर | *gājar* (f) |
| cauliflower | फूलगोभी | *phūlgōbhī* (f) |
| coriander (green) | हरा धनिया | *harā dhaniā* (m) |
| cucumber | खीरा | *khīrā* (m) |
| eggplant, brinjal | बैंगन | *baiñgan* (m) |
| garlic | लहसुन | *lahsun* (m) |
| lime, lemon | नींबू | *nībū* (m) |
| mint | पुदीना | *pudīnā* (m) |
| onion | प्याज़ | *pyāz* (m) |
| okra, Lady's fingers | भिंडी | *bhinḍi* (f) |
| peas | मटर | *maṭar* (f) |
| potato | आलू | *ālū* (m) |
| pumpkin (red) | कद्दू | *kaddū* (m) |

| | | |
|---|---|---|
| radish | मूली | *mūlī* (f) |
| spinach | पालक | *pālak* (m) |
| sweet potato | शकरकंद | *shakarakand* (m) |
| tomato | टमाटर | *ṭamāṭar* (m) |
| turnip | चुकंदर, शलगम | *chukañdar, shalgam* (m) |

**Fruits**—फल

| | | |
|---|---|---|
| apple | सेब | *sēb* (m) |
| apricot | खूबानी | *khūbānī* (f) |
| banana | केला | *kēlā* (m) |
| custard apple | शरीफा | *sharifā* (m) |
| grapes | अंगूर | *angūr* (m) |
| guava | अमरूद | *amrūd* (m) |
| mango | आम | *ām* (m) |
| melon | खरबूजा | *kharbūzā* (m) |
| orange | संतरा | *santarā* (m) |
| papaya | पपीता | *papītā* (m) |
| peach | आड़ू | *āḍū* (m) |
| pear | नाशपाती | *nāshpātī* (m) |
| pineapple | अनान्नास | *anannās* (m) |
| pomegranate | अनार | *anār* (m) |
| watermelon | तरबूज़ | *tarbūz* (m) |

**Spices and condiments**—मसाले वं छौंक

| | | |
|---|---|---|
| aniseed | सौंफ | *sauñf* (m) |
| asafoetida | हींग | *hīng* (f) |
| bayleaf | तेजपत्ता | *tējpattā* (m) |
| cardamom (white) | छोटी इलायची | *chhōṭī elaichī* (f) |
| cardamom (black) | बड़ी इलायची | *baḍī elaichī* (f) |

| | | |
|---|---|---|
| chillies (red) | लाल मिर्च | *lāl mirch* (f) |
| cinnamon | दालचीनी | *dālchīnī* (f) |
| cloves | लौंग | *laung* (m) |
| coriander | धनिया | *dhaniā* (m) |
| cumin | जीरा | *jīrā* (m) |
| fenugreek | मेथी | *mēthī* (f) |
| ginger | अदरक | *adrak* (m) |
| mace | जावित्री | *jāvitrī* (f) |
| mustard | राई | *rāī* (f) |
| nutmeg | जायफल | *jāyphal* (m) |
| pepper (green) | हरी मिर्च | *harī mirch* (f) |
| pepper (black) | काली मिर्च | *kālī mirch* (f) |
| saffron | केसर | *kēsar* (m) |
| salt | नमक | *namak* (m) |
| sesame | तिल | *til* (m) |
| spice | मसाला | *masālā* (m) |
| tamarind | इमली | *imlī* (f) |
| turmeric | हल्दी | *haldī* (f) |

**Weights and measures**—नाप, तौल

| | | |
|---|---|---|
| kilogram | किलोग्राम | *kilō* (m) |
| gram | ग्राम | *grām* (m) |
| scale | तराज़ू | *tarāzū* (f) |
| weight | वज़न | *vazaṇ* (m) |
| heavy | भारी | *bhārī* (ad) |
| light | हल्का | *halka* (ad) |
| litre | लीटर | *liṭar* (m) |
| measurement | नाप, तौल | *nāp, tōl* (m) |
| metre | मीटर | *mītar* (m) |

| | | |
|---|---|---|
| half | आधा | *ādhā* |
| one quarter | चौथाई | *chauthāī* |
| one third | तिहाई | *tihāi* |
| three quarters | तीन चौथाई | *teen-chauthāī* |
| to add | जोड़ना | *jōḍnā* |
| to substract | घटाना | *ghaṭānā* |
| to multiply | गुणा करना | *gunā karnā* |
| to divide | भाग करना | *bhāg karnā* |

**Minerals, metals and precious stones**—खनिज, धातु, रत्न

| | | |
|---|---|---|
| mineral | खनिज | *khanij* (m) |
| metal | धातु | *dhātu* (f) |
| precious stone | रत्न | *ratna* (m) |
| brass | पीतल | *pītal (f)* |
| bronze | कांसा | *kāñsā* (m) |
| copper | तांबा | *tāmbā* (m) |
| gold | सोना | *sōnā* (m) |
| silver | चांदी | *chāñdī* (f) |
| steel | इस्पात | *ispāt* (m) |
| alum | फिटकरी | *phiṭkarī* (f) |
| chalk | खड़िया | *khaḍiyā* (f) |
| clay | मिट्टी | *miṭṭī* (f) |
| glass | शीशा | *shīshā* (m) |
| iron | लोहा | *lōhā* (m) |
| lime | चूना | *chūnā* (m) |
| marble | संगमरमर | *sangmarmar* (m) |
| mercury | पारा | *pārā* (m) |
| coral | मूंगा | *mūñgā* (m) |
| diamond | हीरा | *hīrā* (m) |

| | | |
|---|---|---|
| emerald | पन्ना | *pannā* (m) |
| pearl | मोती | *mōtī* (m) |
| ruby | लाल, माणिक | *lāl, mānik* (m) |

**The house**—मकान

| | | |
|---|---|---|
| bathroom | गुसलखाना | *gusalkhānā* (m) |
| bedroom | सोने का कमरा | *sonē-kā-kamrā* (m) |
| ceiling | छत | *chhat* (m) |
| dining room | खाने का कमरा | *khānē-kā-kamrā* (m) |
| door | दरवाजा | *darvāzā* (m) |
| drawing room | बैठक, बैठने का कमरा | *baithak, baithnē-kā-kamrā* (m) |
| floor | फ़र्श, ज़मीन | *farsh, zamīn* (f) |
| gate | फाटक | *phaṭak* (m) |
| guest room | मेहमान का कमरा | *mēhamān-kā-kamrā* (m) |
| kitchen | रसोईघर | *rasōīghar,* (m), *rasōī* (f) |
| study room | पढ़ने का कमरा | *paḍhnē-kā-kamrā* (m) |
| verandah | बरामदा | *barāmdā* (m) |
| wall | दीवार | *dīvār* (m) |
| window | खिड़की | *khīḍkī* (f) |

**Furniture and furnishings**—फर्नीचर और साज़-सामान

| | | |
|---|---|---|
| bed | पलंग, बिस्तर | *palañg, bistar* (m) |
| carpet | कालीन, गलीचा | *kālīn, galīchā* (m) |
| chair | कुर्सी | *kursī* (f) |
| cupboard | अलमारी | *almārī* (f) |
| curtain | पर्दा | *pardā* (m) |

| | | |
|---|---|---|
| dining table | खाने की मेज़ | *khānē-kī mēz* (f) |
| divan | दीवान | *dīvāān* (m) |
| floor rug | कालीन | *kālīn* (f) |
| mat | चटाई | *chaṭāī* (f) |
| mattress | गद्दा | *gaddā* (m) |
| pillow | तकिया | *takiyā (m)* |
| table | मेज़ | *mēz* (f) |
| table (writing) | लिखने की मेज | *likhnē-kī-mēz* (f) |

**Things around the house**—घर संबंधी वस्तुएं

| | | |
|---|---|---|
| bedcover | पलंगपोश | *palañgposh* (m) |
| bed-sheet | चादर | *chādar* (f) |
| bottle | बोतल | *bōtal* (f) |
| bucket | बाल्टी | *bālṭī* (f) |
| candle | मोमबत्ती | *mōmbattī* (f) |
| key | चाबी | *chābī* (f) |
| lock | ताला | *tālā* (m) |
| mirror | शीशा | *shīshā* (m) |
| needle | सुई | *suī* (f) |
| scissors | कैंची | *kaiñchī* (f) |
| sieve | छलनी | *chhalnī* (f) |
| strainer | छन्नी | *chhannī* (f) |
| thread | धागा | *dhāgā* (m) |
| umbrella | छाता, छतरी | *chhātā, chhatrī* (m) |

**Around the town**—नगर के आसपास

| | | |
|---|---|---|
| airport | हवाई अड्डा | *havāī aḍḍā* (m) |
| building | इमारत, भवन | *imārat* (f) |
| bullock cart | बैलगाड़ी | *bailgāḍī* (f) |

| | | |
|---|---|---|
| church | गिरजाघर | *girjāghar* (m) |
| college | कॉलेज़ | *kālej* (m) |
| crowd | भीड़ | *bhīḍ* (f) |
| ditch | खड्डा, खाई | *khaddā, khaī* (f) |
| electricity | बिजली | *bijlī* (f) |
| farm | खेत, फार्म | *khēt, fārm* |
| fence | बाड़ा | *bāḍa* (m) |
| field | मैदान, खेत | *maidān, khēt* |
| garden | बाग, बगीचा | *bāgh, bagīchā* (m) |
| gutter | नाला | *nālā* (m) |
| hawker | फेरीवाला | *phērīwālā* |
| highway | राजमार्ग | *rajmārg* (f) |
| hospital | अस्पताल | *aspatāl* (m) |
| hotel | होटल | *hōṭal (m)* |
| hut | झोंपड़ी | *jhōñpḍī* |
| inn | सराय | *sarāyē* (f) |
| intersection (roads) | चौराहा | *chaurāhā* (m) |
| land | ज़मीन | *zamīn* (f) |
| lane | गली | *galī* (f) |
| library | पुस्तकालय | *pustakālaya* |
| main market | बड़ा बाजार | *baḍā bāzār* (m) |
| market | बाजार | *bazār* (m) |
| pole (electric) | बिजली का खम्भा | *bijlī-kā-khambhā* |
| post | डाक | *ḍak* (f) |
| postman | डाकिया | *ḍākiyā* (m) |
| post office | डाकघर | *ḍākghar* (m) |
| railway station | रेलवे स्टेशन | *rēlwē sṭēshan* |
| restaurant | रेस्तारॉं | *rēstōrāñ* (m) |
| road | सड़क | *saḍak* (f) |

| | | |
|---|---|---|
| school | स्कूल | *skūl* (m) |
| sewage | नाला | *nālā* (m) |
| shop | दुकान | *dukān* (f) |
| shopkeeper | दुकानदार | *dukāndār* (m) |
| taxi | टैक्सी | *taiksī* |
| telegram | तार | *tār* (m) |
| telegraph office | तारघर | *tārghar* (m) |
| telephone | टेलीफोन | *ṭēlīfōn* (m) |
| university | विश्वविद्यालय | *vishvavidyālaya* (m) |
| zoo | चिड़ियाघर | *chiḍiyāghar* (m) |

**Trades and professions**—व्यापार एवं व्यवसाय

| | | |
|---|---|---|
| artisan | कारीगर | *kārīgar* (m & f) |
| astrologer | ज्योतिषी | *jyotishī* (m & f) |
| author | लेखक | *lekhak, lekhikā* (m), (f) |
| barber | नाई | *nāī* (m) |
| blacksmith | लोहार | *luhār* (m) |
| butcher | कसाई | *kasāī* (m) |
| carpenter | बढ़ई | *baḍhaī* (m) |
| cook | रसोइया, खानसामा | *rasōiyā, khānsāmā* (m) |
| dyer | रंगरेज | *rangrēz* (m) |
| farmer | किसान | *kisān* (m) |
| gardener | माली | *mālī* (m) |
| goldsmith | सुनार | *sunār* (m) |
| jeweller | जौहरी | *jauharī* (m) |
| labourer | मज़दूर | *mazdūr* (m) |
| merchant | व्यापारी | *vyāpārī* (m) |
| milkman | ग्वाला, दूधवाला | *gvālā, dūdhvālā* (m) |

| | | |
|---|---|---|
| nurse | नर्स | *narsa* (f) |
| potter | कुम्हार | *kumhār* |
| servant | नौकर | *naukar* (m) |
| servant (maid) | नौकरानी | *naukarānī* (f) |
| printer | मुद्रक | *mudrak* (m) |
| publisher | प्रकाशक | *prakāshak* (m) |
| sweeper | जमादार | *jamādār* (m) |
| sweet vendor | हलवाई | *halwāī* |
| tailor | दर्ज़ी | *darzī* (m) |
| teacher | शिक्षक, अध्यापक, गुरु | *shikshak* (m) *adhyāpak* (m) *gurū* (m) |
| teacher (lady) | शिक्षिका, अध्यापिका, गुरु | *shikshikā, adhyāpikā, guru* |
| washerman | धोबी | *dhōbi* (m) |
| weaver | जुलाहा, बुनकर | *julāhā, bunkar* (m) |

**The weather–मौसम**

| | | |
|---|---|---|
| rainy season | बरसात | *barsāt* (f) |
| spring | बसंत | *basant* (m) |
| summer | गर्मी | *garmī* (f) |
| winter | जाड़ा | *jāḍā* (m) |
| rain | बारिश | *bārish* (f) |
| duststorm | आंधी | *āndhī* (f) |
| storm | तूफान | *tūfān* (m) |
| wind | हवा | *havā* (f) |
| sun (heat) | धूप | *dhūp* (f) |
| chill | ठंड | *ṭhand* (f) |
| heat | गर्मी | *garmī* (f) |

**Nature**—प्रकृति

| | | |
|---|---|---|
| air | हवा | *havā* (f) |
| atmosphere | वातावरण | *vātāvaraṇ* (m) |
| breeze | हवा | *havā* (f) |
| cliff | चट्टान | *chaṭṭān* (f) |
| cloud | बादल | *bādal* (m) |
| current (river) | धारा | *dhārā* (m) |
| dark night | अंधेरी रात | *andhērī rāt* (m) |
| dawn | प्रातःकाल | *prātakāl* (m) |
| new moon | अमावस | *amāvas* (f) |
| dust | धूल | *dhūl* (f) |
| earth | पृथ्वी | *prithvī* (f) |
| eclipse | ग्रहण | *grahaṇ* (m) |
| fog | कोहरा | *kōhrā* (m) |
| hail | ओला | *ōlā* (m) |
| hill | पहाड़ी | *pahāḍī* |
| lake | झील | *jhīl* (f) |
| light (sun) | सूरज की रोशनी | *sūraj-kī-roshnī* (f) |
| moon | चांद, चंद्रमा | *chāñd, chandrma* (m) |
| moon (full) | पूर्णचंद्र | *pūrṇa chandra* (m) |
| moonlight | चाँदनी | *chāñdnī* (f) |
| moonlit night | चाँदनी रात | *chāñdnī rāt* (f) |
| full-moon night | पूर्णिमा | *pūrṇimā* (f) |
| mountain | पहाड़ | *pahāḍ* (m) |
| ocean | महासागर | *mahāsāgar* (m) |
| peninsula | प्रायद्वीप | *prāyadvīp* (m) |
| rainbow | इन्द्रधनुष | *indradhanush* (m) |
| rainy day | बारिश का दिन | *bārish-kā-din* |
| rock | चट्टान | *chaṭṭān* (f) |

| | | |
|---|---|---|
| sand | बालू | *bālū* (f) |
| sea | समुद्र | *samudra* (m) |
| seaside | समुद्र तट | *samudra-taṭ* |
| sky | आसमान, आकाश | *āsmān, ākāsh* (m) |
| snow | बर्फ़ | *barf* (f) |
| star | तारा | *tārā* (m) |
| wave | लहर | *lahar* (f) |

**Politics, government, etc.**–राजनीति, सरकार आदि

| | | |
|---|---|---|
| administration | प्रशासन | *prashāsan* (m) |
| administrator | प्रशासक | *prashāsak* (m & f) |
| ambassador | राजदूत | *rājdūt* (m & f) |
| democracy | लोकतन्त्र | *loktantra* (m) |
| diplomat | राजनयिक | *rājnayik* (m & f) |
| election | चुनाव | *chunāv* (m) |
| embassy | राजदूतावास | *rājdūtāvās* (m) |
| federation | संघीय | *sanghiya* (m) |
| federal | संघ | *sangh* (m) |
| franchise | मताधिकार | *matādhikār* M) |
| government | सरकार | *sarkār* (f) |
| governmental | सरकारी | *sarkārī* (f) |
| independence | स्वाधीनता | *svādhīntā* (f) |
| imprisonment | क़ैद | *qaid* (f) |
| jail | कारावास | *kārāvās* (m) |
| judge | न्यायाधीश | *nyāyādhish* (m) |
| judgment | फैसला | *faislā* (m) |
| justice | न्याय | *nyāyā* (m) |
| law | कानून | *kānūn* (m) |
| law court | अदालत | *adālat* (f) |

| | | |
|---|---|---|
| law suit | मुक़दमा | *muqadamā* |
| lawyer | वकील | *vakīl* (m & f) |
| legal | कानूनी | *kānūnī* |
| municipality | नगरपालिका | *nagarpālikā* (f) |
| parliament | संसद | *sansad sadasya* |
| Member of Parliament | संसद सदस्य | *sansad sadasya* |
| politics | राजनीति | *rājnīti* (f) |
| political | राजनीतिक | *rājnītik* |
| politician | राजनीतिज्ञ | *rājnītigya* (m&f) |
| vote | मत | *mat* (m) |
| Independence day | स्वाधीनता दिवस | *svādhīntā divas* |
| Republic Day | गणतंत्र दिवस | *gaṇtantra divas* |
| national flag | राष्ट्रीय झंडा | *rāshṭrīya jhaṇḍā* (m) |

**High offices in the country**—देश के प्रमुख पद

| | | |
|---|---|---|
| President | राष्ट्रपति | *rāshṭrapati* |
| Vice-president | उपराष्ट्रपति | *upa-rāshṭrapati* |
| Prime Minister | प्रधान मंत्री | *pradhan mañtri* |
| minister | मंत्री | *mantrī* |
| minister of state | राज्यमंत्री | *rājya-mantrī* |
| deputy minister | उपमंत्री | *upa-mantrī* |
| secretary (to govt.) | सचिव | *sachiva* |
| governor | राज्यपाल | *rājyapāl* |
| President's House | राष्ट्रपति भवन | *rāshṭrapati bhavan* |
| supreme court | सर्वोच्च न्यायालय | *sarvōchcha nyāyālay* |
| chief justice | मुख्य न्यायाधीश | *mukhya nyāyādhīsh* |
| cabinet | मंत्रिमंडल | *mantri-manḍal* |

**Defence**—रक्षा

| | | |
|---|---|---|
| army | सेना | *sēnā* (f) |
| soldier | सैनिक, सिपाही | *sainik, sipāhī* (m) |
| to fight | लड़ाई करना | *laḍāi karnā* |
| war | लड़ाई, युद्ध | *laḍāī, yuddha* (m) |
| peace | शांति | *shānti* (f) |
| weapon | हथियार | *hathiyār* (f) |
| gun | बंदूक | *bandūk* (f) |
| bomb | बम | *bam* (m) |
| truce | संधि | *sandhi* (f) |

**Fine arts, literature etc.**—ललित कलाएं, साहित्य आदि

| | | |
|---|---|---|
| actor | अभिनेता | *abhinētā* (m) |
| actress | अभिनेत्री | *abhinētrī* (f) |
| art | कला | *kalā* (f) |
| artist | कलाकार | *kalākār* (m & f) |
| audience | दर्शक | *darshak* (m) |
| dance | नाच, नृत्य | *nāch, nritya* (m) |
| dancer | नर्तक, नर्तकी नृत्यांगना | *nārtak* (m), *nartakī, nrityan-ganā* (f) |
| drama | नाटक | *nāṭak* (m) |
| dramatist | नाटककार | *nāṭakkār* (m & f) |
| essay | निबंध | *nibandh* (m) |
| essayist | निबंधकार | *nibandhkār* (m & f) |
| folk art | लोककला | *lōk-kala* (f) |
| instrument (musical) | वाद्य | *vādya* |
| music | संगीत | *sangīt* (m) |
| musician | संगीतकार | *sangītkār* (m & f) |

| | | |
|---|---|---|
| novel | उपन्यास | *upanyās* (m) |
| novelist | उपन्यासकार | *upanyāskār* (m& f) |
| poet | कवि | *kavi* (m & f) |
| poetry | कविता | *kavitā* (f) |
| singer | गायक, गायिका | *gāyak* (m), *gāyikā* (f) |
| song | गाना, गीत | *gānā, gīt* (m) |
| song (folk) | लोक गीत | *lokgīt* (f) |
| story (folk) | लोक-कथा | *lok-kathā* (f) |
| story | कहानी | *kahānī* (f) |
| story writer | कहानीकार | *kahānīkār* (m & f) |

**Sports and games**—खेल

| | | |
|---|---|---|
| game | खेल | *khēl* (m) |
| sports | खेल | *khēl* (m) |
| sportsman | खिलाड़ी | *khilāḍī* (m & f) |
| team | टीम | *tīm* (f) |
| group | दल | *dal* (m) |
| playground | खेल का मैदान | *khēl-kā maidān* (m) |
| to win | जीतना | *jītnā* |
| to lose | हारना | *hārnā* |

**Health, illness**—स्वास्थ्य, रोग

| | | |
|---|---|---|
| abdominal pain | पेट का दर्द | *pēt-kā-dard* |
| chicken pox | छोटी माता | *chhōtī mātā* |
| cold | जुकाम | *zukām* |
| cough | खांसी | *khāñsī* |
| fever | बुखार | *bukhār* |
| malaria | मलेरिया | *malēria* |

| | | |
|---|---|---|
| typhoid | मियादी बुखार | *miyādī bukhār* |
| small pox | चेचक | *chēchak* |
| measles | खसरा | *khasrā* |
| pain | दर्द | *dard* |
| swelling | सूजन | *sūjan* |
| medicine | दवा | *davā* |
| medical treatment | इलाज | *ilāj* |
| nausea | जी मचलाना | *jī machlānā* |
| headache | सिर-दर्द | *sir-dard* |
| whooping cough | काली खांसी | *kālī khāñsī* (f) |
| dysentry | पेचिश | *pēchish* (f) |

**Relationship**—संबंध, रिश्ता

| | | |
|---|---|---|
| relationship | रिश्ता, संबंध | *rishtā* |
| relative | रिश्तेदार संबंधी | *rishtēdār* |
| father | पिता, बाप | *pitā, bāp* |
| mother | माँ, माता | *māñ, mātā* |
| brother | भाई | *bhāī* |
| sister | बहिन | *bahin* |
| husband | पति | *pati* |
| wife | पत्नी | *patnī* |
| son | बेटा, पुत्र | *bēṭa, putra* |
| daughter | बेटी, पुत्री | *bēṭī, putrī* |
| nephew (brother's son) | भतीजा | *bhatījā* |
| (sister's son) | भांजा | *bhānjā* |
| niece (brother's daughter) | भतीजी | *bhatījī* |
| (sister's dughter) | भांजी | *bhānjī* |
| uncle (father's brother) | चाचा | *chāchā* |
| (his wife) | चाची | *chāchī* |

| | | |
|---|---|---|
| uncle (mother's brother) | मामा | *māmā* |
| (his wife) | मामी | *māmī* |
| brother-in-law | | |
| (sister's husband) | बहनोई | *bahnōī* |
| (wife's brother) | साला | *sālā* |
| sister-in-law | साली | *sālī* |
| (wife's sister) | | |
| (brother's wife) | भाभी | *bhābhī* |
| father's sister | फूफी | *phūphī* |
| (her husband) | फूफा | *phūphā* |
| grandfather (paternal) | दादा | *dādā* |
| grandmother (paternal) | दादी | *dādī* |
| grandfather (maternal) | नाना | *nānā* |
| grandmother (maternal) | नानी | *nānī* |
| grandson (son's son) | पोता | *pōtā* |
| granddaughter | | |
| (son's daughter) | पोती | *pōtī* |
| grandson | नाती | *nātī* |
| (daughter's son) | | |
| granddaughter | | |
| (daughter's daughter) | नातिन | *nātin* |
| grandchildren | नाती-पोते | *nātī-pōtē* |
| family | परिवार | *parivār* (m) |
| son-in-law | दामाद | *dāmād* |
| daughter-in-law | बहू | *bahū* |
| step-mother | सौतेली माँ | *sautēlī māñ* |
| step-father | सौतेला बाप | *sautēlā bāp* |

**Colours–रंग**

| | | |
|---|---|---|
| black | काला | *kālā* |
| blue | नीला | *nīlā* |
| brown | भूरा | *bhūrā* |
| green | हरा | *harā* |
| pink | गुलाबी | *gulābī* |
| yellow | पीला | *pīlā* |
| olive | मेंहदी | *mēhñdī* |
| orange | नारंगी | *nārangī* |
| purple | बैंगनी | *baiñgni* |
| white | सफेद | *safēd* |

**Adjective–विशेषण (गुणवाचक शब्द)**

| | | |
|---|---|---|
| angry | नाराज | *nārāz* |
| annual | सालाना | *sālānā, vārshik* |
| any | कोई | *koī* |
| bad | बुरा, खराब | *burā, kharāb* |
| beautiful | सुन्दर | *sundar* |
| better | बेहतर, ज़्यादा अच्छा | *bēhtar, zyādā achchhā* |
| big | बड़ा | *baḍā* |
| bitter | कड़ुवा | *kaḍuvā* |
| blind | अंधा | *andhā* |
| boiled | उबला हुआ | *ublā huā* |
| bold | साहसी | *sāhasī* |
| brief | संक्षिप्त | *sañkshipta* |
| broad | चौड़ा | *chauḍā* |
| busy | व्यस्त, मसरूफ़ | *vyast, masrūf* |
| calm | शांत | *shānt* |

| | | |
|---|---|---|
| capable | योग्य, लायक | *yogya, lāyak* |
| careless | लापरवाह | *lāparvāh* |
| central | बीच का, केंद्रीय | *bīch kā, kēndriya* |
| certain | निश्चित | *nishchit* |
| cheap | सस्ता | *sastā* |
| cheerful | खुश, प्रसन्न | *khush, prasanna* |
| clean | साफ़ | *sāf* |
| clear | साफ़ | *sāf* |
| clever | होशियार | *hōshiyār* |
| closed | बंद | *bañd* |
| cold | ठंडा | *ṭhandā* |
| comfortable | आरामदेह | *ārāmdēh* |
| common | आम, सामान्य | *ām, sāmānya* |
| cooked | पका हुआ | *pakā huā* |
| costly | महंगा | *mahañgā* |
| courteous | विनयी | *vinayī* |
| cowardly | डरपोक | *ḍarpōk* |
| damp | गीला | *gīlā* |
| dear (loved one) | प्यारा, प्रिय | *pyārā, priya* |
| decent | अच्छा | *achchhā* |
| deep | गहरा | *gaharā* |
| dense | घना | *ghanā* |
| different | अलग, भिन्न | *alag, bhinna* |
| difficult | कठिन, मुश्किल | *kaṭhin, mushkil* |
| dishonest | बेईमान | *bēīmān* |
| dirty | मैला, गंदा | *mailā, gandā* |
| distant | दूर | *dūr* |
| dry | सूखा | *sūkhā* |

| | | |
|---|---|---|
| dull (slow witted) | बुद्धू | *buddhū* |
| dull (not quick) | सुस्त | *sust* |
| dull (boring) | उबानेवाला | *ubānēvālā* |
| dull (colourless) | फीका | *phīkā* |
| early | शुरू के | *shuru kē* |
| early | जल्दी | *jaldī* |
| easy | आसान | *āsān, saral* |
| economic | आर्थिक | *ārthik* |
| economical (frugal) | किफ़ायतशार | *kifāyatshār* |
| elder | बड़ा | *baḍā* (add *sē* before to denote comparative degree e.g. *ussē baḍā*) |
| empty | खाली | *khālī* |
| enough | काफी | *kāfi* |
| every | हर, प्रति | *har, prati* |
| fair (just) | उचित | *uchit* |
| fair (complexion) | गोरा | *gōrā* |
| fair (weather) | अच्छा, साफ़ | *achchhā, sāf* |
| faithful | वफ़ादार | *vafādār* |
| false | झूठा | *jhūṭhā* |
| famous | मशहूर, प्रसिद्ध | *mashhūr, prasiddha* |
| fat | मोटा | *moṭā* |
| feeble | कमज़ोर | *kamzōr* |
| fertile | उपजाऊ | *upajāū* |
| fierce | भयानक | *bhayānak* |
| happy | सुखी, खुश | *sukhī, khush* |

| | | |
|---|---|---|
| hard | सख्त, कठोर | *sakht, kaṭhōr* |
| harsh | सख्त, कठोर | *sakht, kaṭhōr* |
| hasty | जल्दबाज़ | *jaldbāz* |
| healthy | स्वस्थ, तंदरुस्त | *swasth, tandrust* |
| heavy | भारी | *bhārī* |
| high | ऊंचा | *ūñchā* |
| hollow | पोला | *pōlā* |
| holy | पवित्र | *pavitra* |
| honest | ईमानदार | *īmāndār* |
| hot | गर्म | *garam* |
| humble | नम्र | *namra* |
| ignorant | अज्ञानी | *agyānī* |
| ill | बीमार | *bīmār* |
| imaginary | ख्याली, काल्पनिक | *khyālī, kālpanik* |
| important | ज़रूरी | *zarūrī* |
| innocent (naive) | नादान, भोला | *nādān, bhōlā* |
| innocent (of guilt) | निर्दोष, बेकसूर | *nirdōsh, bēkasūr* |
| insane | पागल | *pāgal* |
| interesting | दिलचस्प, रुचिकर | *dilchasp,ruchi kar* |
| jealous | ईर्ष्यालु | *irshyālu* |
| lame | लंगड़ा | *langḍā* |
| large | बड़ा | *baḍā* |
| last | आखिरी, अंतिम | *ākhirī, antim* |
| late (dead) | स्वर्गीय | *swargīya* |
| late (in time) | देर से | *dēr sē* |
| lazy | आलसी, सुस्त | *ālsī, sust* |
| lean | दुबला | *dublā* |
| learned | विद्वान | *vidvān* |

| | | |
|---|---|---|
| light (weight) | हल्का | *halkā* |
| little (size) | छोटा | *chhoṭā* |
| little (quantity) | थोड़ा | *thoḍā* |
| long | लम्बा | *lambā* |
| low | नीचा | *nīchā* |
| mad | पागल | *pāgal* |
| many | बहुत | *bahut* |
| mean (person's behaviour) | नीच | *nīch* |
| moral | नैतिक | *naitik* |
| much | बहुत | *bahut* |
| narrow | तंग, सँकरा | *tang, sañkrā* |
| national | राष्ट्रीय | *rashṭrīya* |
| natural | कुदरती | *kudaratī* |
| necessary | जरूरी | *zarūrī* |
| next | दूसरा, अगला | *dūsrā, aglā* |
| new | नया | *nayā* |
| notorious | बदनाम | *badnām* |
| obedient | आज्ञाकारी | *āgyākārī* |
| official | सरकारी | *sarkārī* |
| old (opp. of new) | पुराना | *purānā* |
| old (age) | बूढ़ा, बुड्ढा | *buḍḍhā* |
| only | केवल, सिर्फ | *kēval, sirf* |
| open | खुला | *khulā* |
| other | दूसरा | *dūsarā* |
| patient | सब्रदार, धैर्यवान | *sabradār, dhairyavān* |
| peaceful | शान्त | *shānt* |
| quiet | शान्त | *shānt* |
| rapid | तेज़ | *tēz* |

| | | |
|---|---|---|
| raw | कच्चा | *kachchā* |
| real | सच्चा, असली | *sachchā, aslī* |
| religious | धार्मिक | *dhārmik* |
| respectful | सम्मानपूर्ण | *sammānpūrṇa* |
| respected | सम्मानित | *sammānit* |
| rich | अमीर, धनी | *amīr, dhanī* |
| right (correct) | ठीक | *ṭhīk* |
| right (hand) | दाहिना, दायां | *dāhinā, dāyāñ* |
| ripe | पक्का, पका | *pakkā, pakā* |
| rough (texture) | खुरदरा | *khurdurā* |
| round | गोल | *gōl* |
| rude | बदतमीज़ | *badtamīz* |
| rural | देहांती | *dēhātī* |
| sacred | पवित्र | *pavitra* |
| sad | उदास, दुखी | *udās, dukhī* |
| safe | सुरक्षित | *surakshit* |
| same | वही, वैसा ही | *vahī, vaisā hī* |
| secret | गुप्त, रहस्य | *gupta, rahasya* |
| severe | सख्त, कठोर | *sakht, kaṭhōr* |
| shallow | छिछला | *chhichhlā* |
| sharp | तेज़ | *tēz* |
| short (brief) | छोटा, संक्षिप्त | *chhōtā,* |
| short (stature) | नाटा | *nāṭā* |
| silken | रेशमी | *reshamī* |
| slow (speed) | धीरे | *dhīrē* |
| slow (backward not smart) | पीछे, सुस्त | *pīchhē, sust* |
| small | छोटा | *chhōṭā* |
| social | सामाजिक | *sāmājik* |

| | | |
|---|---|---|
| soft | नर्म, मुलायम | *narm, mulāyam* |
| solid | ठोस | *ṭhōs* |
| some | कुछ | *kuchh* |
| sour | खट्टा | *khaṭṭā* |
| special | खास | *khās* |
| stale | बासी | *bāsī* |
| strange | विचित्र, अजीब | *vichitra, ajīb* |
| strong | मज़बूत | *mazbūt* |
| stupid | बेवकूफ, मूर्ख | *bevakūf, mūrkh* |
| successful | सफल | *saphal* |
| such | ऐसा | *aisā* |
| sure | निश्चित, निश्चय | *nishchit, nishchaya* |
| sweet | मीठा | *mīṭhā* |
| swift | तेज़ | *tēz* |
| tasty | स्वादिष्ट | *svādishṭ* |
| tender | नर्म, मुलायम | *narm, mulāyam* |
| thick | मोटा | *moṭā* |
| thin (person, animal) | दुबला | *dublā* |
| thin (neuter gender) | पतला | *patlā* |
| thirsty | प्यासा | *pyāsā* |
| tight | तंग, कसा | *tang, kasā* |
| tired | थका | *thakā* |
| true | सच | *sach* |
| ugly | बदसूरत | *badsūrat* |
| vain | घमंडी | *ghamanḍī* |
| weak | कमजोर | *kamzōr* |
| wily | चालाक | *chālāk* |
| wise | बुद्धिमान | *buddhimān* |

| | | |
|---|---|---|
| zealous | उत्साही | *utsāhī* |

**Verbs**—क्रियायें

| | | |
|---|---|---|
| to accept | मंजूर करना<br>स्वीकार | *manzūr karnā,*<br>*svīkār karnā* |
| to admire | प्रशंसा करना | *prashansā karnā* |
| to advise | सलाह देना,<br>राय देना | *salāh dēnā, rāyē*<br>*dēnā* |
| to answer | जवाब देना | *javāb dēnā* |
| to argue | बहस करना | *bahas karnā* |
| to arrange | इंतज़ाम करना | *intazām karnā* |
| to arrive | पहुंचना | *pahuñchnā* |
| to arrest | गिरफ्तार करना | *gìrftār karnā* |
| to ask | पूछना | *pūchhnā* |
| to attack | हमला करना | *hamlā karnā* |
| to attempt | कोशिश करना | *kōshish karnā* |
| to awake | जागना, जगाना | *jāganā, jagānā* |
| to be | होना | *hōnā* |
| to be afraid | डरना | *ḍarnā* |
| to be angry | नाराज़ होना,<br>गुस्सा करना | *nārāz hōnā,*<br>*gussā karnā* |
| to be tired | थकना | *thaknā* |
| to bathe | नहाना, स्नान करना | *nahānā, snān*<br>*karnā* |
| to bear (tolerate) | सहना | *sahnā* |
| to bear the burden | भार उठाना | *bhār uṭhānā* |
| to become | होना, हो जाना | *hōnā, hō jānā* |
| to beat | मारना, पीटना | *mārnā, pīṭnā* |
| to beat (egg) | फेटना | *phēñṭnā* |

| | | |
|---|---|---|
| to beg | भीख मांगना | *bhīkh māñgnā* |
| to begin | शुरु करना | *shurū karnā* |
| to believe | विश्वास करना | *vishvās karnā* |
| to bite | काटना | *kāṭnā* |
| to blame | दोष देना | *dōsh dēnā* |
| to boil (tr.) | उबालना | *ubālnā* |
| to boil (int.) | उबलना | *ubalnā* |
| to break (tr.) | तोड़ना | *tōṛnā* |
| to break (int.) | टूटना | *ṭūṭnā* |
| to breathe | सांस लेना | *sāñs lēnā* |
| to bring | लाना | *lānā* |
| to build | बनाना | *banānā* |
| to burn (int.) | जलना | *jalnā* |
| to burst (tr.) | फाड़ना | *phāḍnā* |
| to burst (int.) | फटना | *phaṭnā* |
| to buy | खरीदना | *kharīdnā* |
| to call | बुलाना | *bulānā* |
| to care | परवाह करना | *parvāḥ karnā* |
| to carry | उठाना | *uṭhānā* |
| to catch | पकड़ना | *pakaḍnā* |
| to change | बदलना | *badalnā* |
| to change (int.) | बदल जाना | *badal jānā* |
| to chop | छोटे टुकड़े काटना | *chhōṭē tukḍē kāṭnā* |
| to clean | साफ़ करना | *sāf karnā* |
| to climb | चढ़ना | *chaḍhnā* |
| to desire | चाहना | *chāhnā* |
| to die | मरना | *marnā* |
| to dig | खोदना | *khōdnā* |

| | | |
|---|---|---|
| to do | करना | *karnā* |
| to doubt | शक करना, संदेह करना | *shak karnā, sandeh karnā* |
| to draw | खींचना | *khīñchnā* |
| to dream | सपना देखना | *sapnā dēkhnā* |
| to dress | कपड़े पहनना | *kapdē pahannā* |
| to drink | पीना | *pīnā* |
| to drive (a car) | मोटर चलाना | *motar chalānā* |
| to dry (tr.) | सुखाना | *sukhānā* |
| to dry (int.) | सूखना | *sūkhanā* |
| to eat | खाना | *khānā* |
| to exclaim | चिल्लाना | *chillānā* |
| to explain | समझाना | *samjhānā* |
| to excuse | माफ करना | *māf karnā* |
| to examine | परीक्षण करना, जांचना | *parikshan karna, jānchnā* |
| to fall | गिरना | *girnā* |
| to fear | डरना | *ḍarnā* |
| to feed | खिलाना | *khilānā* |
| to feel | अनुभव करना | *anubhava karnā* |
| to fight | लड़ना | *laḍnā* |
| to fill | भरना | *bharnā* |
| to find | पाना | *pānā* |
| to finish | ख़त्म करना | *khatm karnā* |
| to forget | भूलना | *bhūlnā* |
| to forgive | माफ़ करना | *māf karnā* |
| to freeze | जमाना | *jamānā* |
| to freeze (int.) | जमना | *jamnā* |
| to fry | तलना | *talnā* |

| | | |
|---|---|---|
| to get | पाना | *pānā* |
| to get up | उठना | *uṭhnā* |
| to give | देना | *dēnā* |
| to give up | छोड़ देना | *chhōḍ dēnā* |
| to go | जाना | *jānā* |
| to go in | अंदर जाना | *andar jānā* |
| to go out | बाहर आना | *bāhar jānā* |
| to get out | बाहर निकलना | *bāhar nikalnā* |
| to grind | पीसना | *pīsnā* |
| to grow | बढ़ना | *baḍhnā* |
| to guide | रास्ता दिखाना | *rāstā dikhānā* |
| to increase | बढ़ाना | *baḍhānā* |
| to insult | अपमान करना | *apmān karnā* |
| to irrigate | सींचना | *sīchnā* |
| to irritate | नाराज़ करना | *nārāz karnā* |
| to introduce | परिचय कराना | *parichay karānā* |
| to joke | मज़ाक करना | *mazāk karnnā* |
| to jump | कूदना | *kūdanā* |
| to keep | रखना | *rakhnā* |
| to kick | लात मारना | *lāt mārnā* |
| to kill | जान से मारना<br>मार डालना | *jān sē mārnā,*<br>*mār ḍālnā* |
| to kiss | चूमना | *chūmna* |
| to know | जानना | *jānanā* |
| to laugh | हंसना | *hañsnā* |
| to lay the table | मेज़ लगाना | *mēz lagānā* |
| to lead (the way) | रास्ता दिखाना,<br>आगे आगे चलना | *rāstā dikhānā,*<br>*āgē-āgē chalnā* |
| to learn | सीखना | *sīkhnā* |

| | | |
|---|---|---|
| to lend | उधार देना | *udhār dēnā* |
| to lie down | लेटना | *lēṭnā* |
| to lie (telling) | झूठ बोलना | *jhūṭh bōlnā* |
| to lift | उठाना | *uṭhānā* |
| to like | पसंद करना | *pasand karnā* |
| to look | देखना | *dēkhnā* |
| to lose | खोना | *khōnā* |
| to love | प्यार करना | *pyār karnā* |
| to make | बनाना | *banānā* |
| to marry | शादी करना | *shādī karnā* |
| to measure | नापना, तोलना | *nāpnā, taulnā* |
| to meet | मिलना | *milnā* |
| to memorize | रटना | *raṭnā* |
| to move (tr.) | सरकाना | *sarakānā* |
| to move on | आगे सरकना | *āgē sarkanā* |
| to obey | कहना मानना, आज्ञा मानना, | *kahnā mānanā, āgyā mānnaā* |
| to object | आपत्ति करना | *āpatti karnā* |
| to offend | नाराज़ करना | *nārāz karnā* |
| to open | खोलना | *khōlnā* |
| to open (in.) | खुलना | *khulnā* |
| to order | आज्ञा देना | *āgyā dēnā* |
| to paint (to colour) | रंगना, रंग करना | *rangnā, rang karnā* |
| to paint a picture | चित्र बनाना | *chitra banānā* |
| to raise | उठाना | *uṭhānā* |
| to read | पढ़ना | *paḍhnā* |
| to receive | पाना | *pānā* |
| to recommend | सिफारिश करना | *sifārish karnā* |

| | | |
|---|---|---|
| to refuse | मना करना | *manā karnā* |
| to regret | अफ़सोस करना | *afsōs karnā* |
| to reject | अस्वीकार करना | *asvīkār karnā* |
| to remember | याद करना | *yād karnā* |
| to rest | आराम करना | *ārām karnā* |
| to return | लौटाना | *lauṭānā* |
| to return (int.) | लौटना | *lauṭanā* |
| to ring (bell) | घंटी बजाना | *ghanṭī bajānā* |
| to ride | सवार होना | *savār hōnā* |
| to rinse | धोना | *dhōnā* |
| to roast | भूनना | *bhūnanā* |
| to run | दौड़ना | *dauḍnā* |
| to run away | भाग जाना | *bhāg jānā* |
| to say | कहना | *kahnā* |
| to scold | डांटना | *ḍañṭnā* |
| to search | ढूंढ़ना, खोजना | *ḍhunḍhanā, khōjnā* |
| to see | देखना | *dēkhnā* |
| to sell | बेचना | *bēchnā* |
| to send | भेजना | *bhējnā* |
| to send for | बुला भेजना | *bulā bhējnā* |
| to serve | सेवा करना | *sēvā karnā* |
| to sew | सीना | *sīnā* |
| to shake | हिलाना | *hilānā* |
| to shake (int.) | हिलना | *hilnā* |
| to shake hands | हाथ मिलाना | *hāth milānā* |
| to shave | दाढ़ी बनाना | *dāḍhī banānā* |
| to shout | चिल्लाना | *chillānā* |
| to show | दिखाना | *dikhānā* |

| | | |
|---|---|---|
| to sing | गाना | *gānā* |
| to sink | डूबना | *ḍūbanā* |
| to sit | बैठना | *baiṭhanā* |
| to sleep | सोना | *sōnā* |
| to (put to) sleep | सुलाना | *sulānā* |
| to smell | सूंघना | *sūnghana* |
| to smile | मुस्कराना | *muskarānā* |
| to sneeze | छींकना | *chhīñknā* |
| to sow | बोना | *bōnā* |
| to speak | बोलना | *bōlnā* |
| to spit | थूकना | *thūknā* |
| to stand | खड़ा होना | *khaḍā hōnā* |
| to stay | ठहरना | *ṭhaharanā* |
| to steal | चुराना, चोरी करना | *churānā, chōri karnā* |
| to stop | रुकना | *ruknā* |
| to strike | मारना | *mārnā* |
| to strike (work) | हड़ताल करना | *haṛtāl karnā* |
| to study | पढ़ना | *paḍhnā* |
| to suspect | शक करना | *shak karnā* |
| to swear | कसम खाना | *kasam khānā* |
| to swear (abuse) | गाली देना | *gālī dēnā* |
| to swim | तैरना | *tairnā* |
| to take | लेना | *lēnā* |
| to taste | चखना | *chakhnā* |
| to tear | फाड़ना | *phāḍnā* |
| to tell | बताना | *batānā* |
| to think | सोचना | *sōchnā* |
| to try | कोशिश करना | *kōshish karnā* |

| | | |
|---|---|---|
| to thank | धन्यवाद देना | *dhanyavād dēnā* |
| to throw | फेंकना | *phēñknā* |
| to tighten | कसना | *kasnā* |
| to translate | अनुवाद करना | *anuvād karnā* |
| to understand | समझना | *samajhnā* |
| to undress | कपड़े उतारना | *kapḍē utārnā* |
| to use | इस्तेमाल करना, उपयोग करना | *istēmāl karnā, upyōg karnā* |
| to utter | कहना | *kahnā* |
| to walk | चलना | *chalnā* |
| to walk for pleasure | सैर करना | *sair karnā* |
| to want | चाहना | *chāhnā* |
| to wash | धोना | *dhōnā* |
| to waste | बर्बाद करना | *barbād karnā* |
| to water (the plants) | पानी देना | *pānī dēnā* |
| to wear | पहनना | *pahananā* |
| to weave | बुनना | *bunanā* |
| to weep | रोना | *rōnā* |
| to weigh | तौलना | *tōlnā* |
| to whistle | सीटी बजाना | *sīṭī bajānā* |
| to wish | चाहना | *chāhnā* |
| to win | जीतना | *jītanā* |
| to work | काम करना | *kām karnā* |
| to write | लिखना | *likhnā* |
| to yell | चिल्लाना | *chillānā* |

**Some other useful words and phrases**

| | | |
|---|---|---|
| to finish (int.) | ख़त्म होना | *khatm hōnā* |
| to finish (tr.) | ख़त्म करना | *khatm karnā* |

| | | |
|---|---|---|
| specially, particularly | खासकर | *khās kar* |
| please excuse me | क्षमा कीजिए, माफ कीजिए | *kshamā kījiyē, māf kījiyē* |
| sorry, I am late | अफ़सोस है, देर हो गयी | *afsōs hai, dēr hō gayī* |
| I am early | मैं जल्दी आ गया | *maiñ jaldī ā gayā* |
| does not matter | कोई बात नहीं | *kōī bāt nahīñ* |
| please don't mind | बुरा न मानिए | *burā nā māniyē* |
| please | कृपया, कृपा करके, मेहरबानी से | *kirpayā, kirpā kar kē, meharbānī sē* |
| to put on shoes | जूते पहनना | *jūtā pahnanā* |
| to celebrate | खुशी मनाना, उत्सव मनाना | *khushī manānā, utsava manānā* |
| to congratulate | बधाई देना, मुबारकबाद देना | *badhāī dēnā, mubārakabād dēnā* |
| congratulations | बधाई, मुबारकबाद | *badhāī, mubārakabād* |
| happy new year | नया साल मुबारक हो | *nayā sāl mubārak hō* |
| best wishes for birthday | जन्मदिन मुबारक हो | *janmadin mubārak hō* |
| good wishes | शुभ कामनाएं | *shubh kāmanāēñ* |

**Various uses of the word** *tēz*

| | | |
|---|---|---|
| The fever is high. | बुखार तेज़ है। | *bukhār tēz hai* |
| The sun is strong. | धूप तेज़ है। | *dhūp tēz hai* |
| The knife is sharp. | छरी तेज़ है। | *chhurī tēz hai* |

| | | |
|---|---|---|
| The boy is sharp. (int) | लड़का तेज़ है। | *laḍkā tēz hai* |
| The light is strong. | रोशनी तेज़ है। | *roshnī tēz hai* |
| The wind is strong. | हवा तेज़ है। | *havā tēz hai* |
| He runs fast. | वह तेज़ दौड़ता है। | *vah tēz dauḍatā hai* |
| Take tea after taking the medicine. | दबा खाकर चाय पीजिए। | *davā khākar chāyē pījiyē* |
| Sleep after eating. | खाना खाकर सो जाइए | *khānā khākar sō jaiyē* |
| I shall go for a walk after dinner. | मैं खाना खाकर घूमने जाऊंगा | *māiñ khānā ghūmane jāūñgā* |
| After reading tell me how the book is. | पढ़कर बताइए यह किताब कैसी है | *paḍh kar batāiyē yah kitāb kaisi hai* |

**Cooking**—पाक शास्त्र

| | | |
|---|---|---|
| to bake | सेंकना | *sēñkanā* |
| to boil | उबालना | *ubālnā* |
| to chill | ठंडा करना | *thanḍā karnā* |
| to chop | छोटे टुकड़े करना | *chhoṭē tukdē karnā* |
| to cut | काटना | *kaṭnā* |
| to cover | ढकना | *ḍhaknā* |
| to dice | टुकड़े काटना | *tukṛē kātanā* |
| to fry | तलना | *talnā* |
| to grate | कसना | *kasnā* |
| to grind | पीसना | *pīsnā* |
| to freeze | जमाना | *jamānā* |
| to mash | मसलना | *masalnā* |
| to peel | छीलना | *chhilnā* |

| | | |
|---|---|---|
| to scrape | खुरचना | *khurachanā* |
| spices | मसाले | *masālē* |
| to strain | छानना | *chhānanā* |
| to season | तड़का देना | *taḍkā dēnā* |
| to warm up | गरम करना | *garam karnā* |
| to wash | धोना | *dhōnā* |

**The 'Wallah'**

Some foreigners living in India have adopted the word 'wallah' to mean a hawker. Actually the word spelt phonetically is *vālā,* and by itself it does not have any meaning, but when combined with other words it has a variety of meanings. For example, when combined with the name of a commodity it would mean the seller of the particular commodity, e. g.,

| | |
|---|---|
| *sabzīvālā* | vegetable vendor |
| *phalvālā* | fruit vendor |
| *phūlvālā* | flower vendor |
| *kapḍēvālā* | cloth vendor |
| *bartanvālā* | utensil vendor |
| *akhbārvālā* | newspaperman |
| *dūdhvālā* | milkman |
| *khilaunēvālā* | toy-seller |
| *taxīvālā* | taxi driver |

But that is not all. *vālā* may be combined with the name of a city or town to mean a person belonging to that place, e.g., *Dillivālā, Bambaīvālā* and so on.

*Vālā* is also used to specify a certain thing. For example

*kalvālā akhbār* means yesterday's newspaper; *ūparvālā kamrā* means the room upstairs. The meaning would be the same if you said *kal kā akhbār* or *upār kamrā*, but *vālā* is idiomatic and a colloquial expression.

32 pages of 'A tourist Guide to Dialogues' continues after these 6 pages of notes.

## *Notes*

# Notes

# Notes

# Notes